BUSINESS BEYOND THE BOX

BUSINESS BEYOND THE BOX

Applying Your Mind for Breakthrough Results

John O'Keeffe

NICHOLAS BREALEY
PUBLISHING
LONDON

First published by
Nicholas Brealey Publishing Limited in 1998

36 John Street	671 Clover Drive
London	Santa Rosa
WC1A 2AT, UK	CA 95401, USA
Tel: +44 (0)171 430 0224	Tel: (707) 566 8006
Fax: +44 (0)171 404 8311	*Fax: (707) 566 8005*

http://www.nbrealey-books.com

Library of Congress Cataloging in Publication Data applied for

ISBN 1-85788-212-1

British Library Cataloguing in Publication Data
A catalogue record for this book is available from the British Library.

Printed in Finland by Werner Söderström Oy.

Contents

Foreword

The exact expressions of this book's concepts have resulted from several years of practicing what I preach and preaching what I practice. So my thanks cover several stages of evolution.

For giving me the inspiration to write, thanks to Steven Covey who taught me third-party teaching: that the way to get brilliant at something is to commit to subsequently teach it to others.

For stretching me further, thank you to Karen O'Donnell of Management Centre Europe, for persuading me to take days off on vacation and present the concepts on the same platform as the likes of Peter Drucker, Michael Porter, Gary Hamel and Sumantra Ghoshal. There's nothing like competition to sharpen one's focus.

For finding the time to put it down in writing, while simultaneously pursuing a line management career with Procter & Gamble, some special thanks: to slow room services in the world's hotels on nights away from home; to passengers next to me on flights who tolerated an anti-social neighbor; to air-traffic control and the airlines for all the delays; and to time zones and jet lag that often kept me awake at 3 in the morning.

In finalizing the book I'm very grateful to Sally Lansdell who has taken my timber and with deft touches helped turn it into polished wood. But mostly to Nick Brealey, my publisher, who has pushed, stimulated and challenged me to make the good better, the clear more vivid and the provocative even more relevant.

My last words of thanks go to my family. My children, Tim, Sam and Kelly, have gleefully mocked my worst thoughts and helped mold my best ideas. Jeannie, my wife and best friend, has given me sustained encouragement over the years and helped give me the resolve to keep at it, which is worth so much to any writer but not least to one with a day job. Without her support this book simply wouldn't have happened.

John O'Keeffe
April 1998

Let's admit it. Corporations around the world are reaching the limits of incrementalism. Squeezing another penny out of costs, getting a product to market a few weeks earlier, responding to customers' enquiries a little bit faster, ratcheting quality up one more notch, capturing another point of market share – those are the obsessions of managers today. But pursuing incremental improvements, while rivals reinvent the industry, is like fiddling while Rome burns.

Gary Hamel, Strategy as Revolution

1

Business Beyond the Box

This book will help you achieve breakthrough results in whatever you do. It will give you the secrets of operating beyond the box of conventional thinking habits and mindsets.

But *Business Beyond the Box* is far more than just 'thinking out of the box'. It is far more than creative thinking. *Business Beyond the Box* is about both applying your mind *and* achieving breakthrough, step-change business results.

This book is about developing the ability to create a flow of ideas that will bring about a step-change in actual results — not impractical, blue-sky ideas that don't work, but step-change ideas that bring step-change results. These can be great ideas that result in step-change products, step-change ways of marketing, step-change ways to serve customers, step-change ways to make money, step-change improvements to any part of an operation.

This book is about you and your organization's ability to innovate, rather than administrate; challenge the status quo, rather than accept it; to look at what can be, rather than what is; to play *with* boundaries, rather than play *within* boundaries.

The book is a step-change in itself. It takes the major strategic thrusts of key management thinkers and practitioners, like the ones at the beginning of each chapter, and transforms them into eight practical strategies on which everyone can take action day to day.

The eight thinking strategies outlined in this book can be put into practice by any manager to achieve step-change results in his or her area. You don't have to wait for the whole organization to 'convert' – whoever you are, at whatever level, you can start reaping rich rewards by applying these strategies within your own sphere of influence.

Get beyond the box of incrementalism

The box of incrementalism – aiming only for minor improvements on past performance – is formed by satisfaction with the status quo, by self-imposed limitations you hardly realize are there, and by a habit of seeking only modest changes to whatever you have.

The rate of change is now so high that incrementalism will not work, let alone maximize your potential. Individuals and organizations could previously gain a competitive edge by developing a slightly better way of doing things. Indeed, things were static for so long that the change did not need to be that big to have an impact.

Now it is different. We need to get out of our boxes just to find some way of coping with the changes taking place around our business, let alone to develop a competitive edge for the future. Staying comfortably in the 'box of incrementalism' will lead to failure. It's like being faced with a galeforce wind. If you aim to take a small step forward you will probably end up by going backwards. You need to take a big step into the teeth of the gale merely to hold your position.

The past should be a springboard. Too many organizations use it as a sofa. Does your organization use it more like a springboard or more like a sofa?

Business-as-usual is no longer a strategy for success – the usual is no longer usual. It rapidly becomes out of date. And the rate of change offers opportunities for competition to exploit, if you fail to do so. But organizations and people get stuck in the box of incrementalism because of the fear of upsetting an operation that has worked well in the past, even though that past will not be repeated in the future.

Under an incrementalist approach you set out to be just a little better than you are – and that is a self-imposed limit to how much better you can be. If you adopt incrementalism you accept your current situation, you will be satisfied with only a small improvement over the status quo. But when tomorrow is so different to today, incrementalism may not even bring any improvement. In contrast, by following the strategies in this book you will be able to break out of the box of incrementalism, change your restrictive thought processes and adopt new mindsets that will bring step-change, breakthrough results.

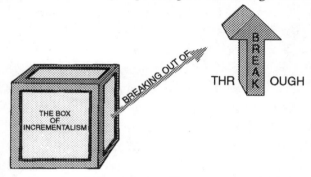

This books seeks a breakthrough in effectiveness for managers. Many traditional books and articles give detailed case histories of businesses which have achieved step-changes rather than settling for modest improvements on traditional methods. So the management theories and commentaries tend to focus on how, for example, CNN achieved a breakthrough on news delivery; Direct Line achieved a breakthrough in insurance; SAP achieved a breakthrough in data exchange; Dell Computers achieved a breakthrough in computer delivery; Federal Express achieved a breakthrough in parcel delivery; Calloway achieved a breakthrough in golf equipment; Honda outstripped Volkswagen; Glaxo beat Upjohn; CNN won over CBS; Canon overtook Xerox; British Airways beat Pan Am.

And similar books document the breakthroughs achieved by the Body Shop, Walmart, Benetton, Nike, Sony and Netscape. And we also learn about the 'innovation culture' at companies like 3M or Hallmark.

All these tend to be stories of breakthroughs in the organizations' principal products or services. However, in practice, the focus on breakthrough rather than incrementalism can be applied successfully to a wider range of business parameters – with huge beneficial effects on the bottom line. For example, you might develop breakthrough ways to double prices, halve a cost, achieve a step-change in sales growth, triple line-speeds, make a process obsolete or transform the entire organization.

And case histories tend to be after-the-fact observations – that's easy. The key trick is to generate before-the-fact changes in habits and thinking strategies that will lead to breakthrough results.

Moreover, brilliant step-change results can come from each and every manager adopting new thinking strategies. But for the vast majority of managers and organizations, the literature isn't practical enough. It is aimed too much at the occasional boardroom big play. The focus is on mega-deals or mega-transformations that only senior managers can carry out – like divestitures, acquisitions or reengineering – or those that require setting up a major change program, sending everyone on training courses or bringing in a team of consultants.

Business Beyond the Box is a breakthrough book because the strategies it outlines are surprisingly effective at getting step-change results from relatively easy changes that most people can make. It aims to answer the question: 'What can I do *now* to achieve breakthrough results in my business area?'

Breakthrough results, relatively easily

The techniques in this book work for three reasons:

Monday morning do-able

These techniques are user friendly. The book provides many simple examples, tips and exercises to bring the methods to life. They will be quickly transmitted through the organization because they are practical, amusing and stimulating. Each and every person in the organization can use them.

Too many programs and techniques require a wholesale conversion from one approach to another – they are all or nothing. This book is different. Not all of it has to be applied to everything from day one. You'll find that even 5 or 10 percent of the techniques applied 20 or 30 percent of the time can, and will, dramatically change your results.

View this book as a handbook for your cranial computer to be used by everyone from the chairman to the first-level manager. And to help spread the techniques there is some 'software' at the back of the book to help put the thinking strategies into operation.

Direct to results

These strategies focus each individual's thinking and energies *directly* on how to get breakthrough results. This contrasts with many of today's activities where our thinking and energy are taken up with activities like teambuilding, skill training, motivation, empowerment or reward systems.

All of these are helpful, but are essentially tangential in their contribution to step-change results. A significant change in one of these tangential areas may still yield only a small improvement in bottom-line results. Indeed, even with a major improvement in such an area, it is often difficult to see its effect on the bottom line.

By contrast, a sustained focus on breakthrough results will develop different changes. How can we double the profit, double sales, halve the cost, halve the time to market, double the output etc.?

Proven in practice

The proof of the pudding is in the eating. The strategies come straight from the horse's mouth of a practicing senior line executive in a major multinational company.

In my 25 years with Procter & Gamble I've had a variety of line jobs, from Europe to the Middle East to the Far East to the US. In a relatively short space of time I've taken losing businesses and turned them round; achieved step-change in market share; taken businesses with a satisfactory level of performance and supercharged them; and transformed business portfolios.

The theme of whatever success I've achieved has not been better management, better administration or incremental improvements. The theme of my success has been getting organizations to cut loose from the limited mindsets of the present and the past and adopt new mindsets to bring breakthrough success in the future.

This book is about helping you to follow this process for yourself. The methods were put into operation last week and the week before, and they will still be put into practice next week and the week after. These are not theoretical models, derived from analysis by a business school or consultant. Indeed, these techniques take the broad, theoretical models and bring them down to the practical action that each and every individual can take to help get breakthrough results.

Business beyond the box in the real world

What is your real world like now? If you are a member of a large organization, your day is likely to be a cobweb of handling in-trays or e-mails, writing reports or memos, a series of formal and informal meetings with one other person or in a group or team, visits to suppliers, plants, customers, buyers and other parts of your organization.

You will be operating a cobweb of processes full of budgets, measures and targets, perhaps weekly, monthly and yearly. You'll have agendas and project lists, reviews and presentations. Your diary may well be full. You will be busy, with your days filled up with similar activities to last year and the year before.

You'll have hopes of recognition of your work and your results, and hopes of salary increases or promotion. Your success is probably measured by how well you manage this cobweb of processes to produce incrementally better results than before and better results than others with whom you are competing.

The good news is that you don't necessarily need to change the cobweb of processes to achieve discontinuous results – results that achieve a step-change beyond the box – just change some habits within the cobweb.

Most of your time and talent in the cobweb are currently destined to produce only incrementally better results. Simply decide from now on to spend only 50 percent of your time on incremental activities and to invest the remaining 50 percent in applying the methods and strategies for breakthrough results.

So, in a meeting, spend only half the time on making sure that this month's and this year's activities are in place, ensuring that you are on track and debating relatively minor improvements to the current state. And in the remaining half of the time focus on the techniques for achieving step-change, breakthrough results. The same applies to business reviews, report writing, visits, presentations and so on.

How important is business beyond the box?

Imagine the establishment of an independent 'Business Beyond the Box Institute' whose primary function is to grant companies a rating, in much the same way as banks and financial institutes allocate credit ratings.

Clearly, every company would want a high 'business beyond the box' rating. And investors would prefer to buy the stocks and shares of these companies with high ratings and their stock or share price would rise proportionately.

The techniques in this book are designed to help you get a high 'business beyond the box' rating. How far you are able to go beyond the box will define your ability to succeed in the future through gaining a competitive edge.

That's how important it is.

THE EIGHT THINKING STRATEGIES

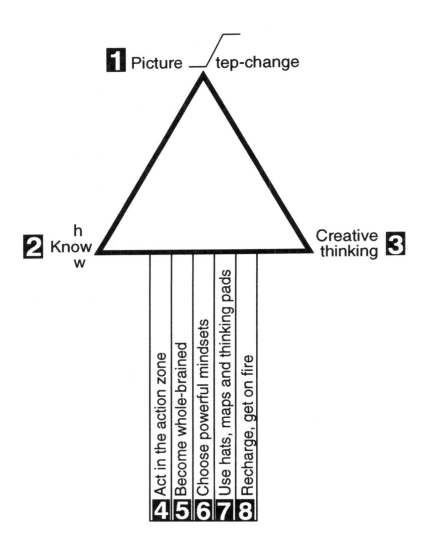

2 The Eight Thinking Strategies

The major challenge for leaders in the twenty-first century will be how to release the brain power of their organizations.

Warren Bennis

How can you get the breakthrough results you need? The answer lies in eight new thinking strategies for yourself and others around you, with tools and techniques that anyone can use in support of them.

Business Beyond the Box takes a bottom–line approach. It is about applying your mind to achieve real, step-change results.

Your mind is a brilliant personal cranial computer but most people don't know how to operate it. Indeed, other than using their mind to plough through lots of analytical thinking, most people don't have a clue what else to do with it. The only other strategy than analytical thinking that gets used is a vague form of something called brain-storming, which often ends up as some sideshow frivolity that is rarely practical in practice.

Using your cranial computer only for analytical thinking is the equivalent of having the most powerful laptop computer and just using it for wordprocessing. And letting the only other alternative strategy be brainstorming or wild creative thinking is the equivalent of using the most powerful laptop for an elementary electronic game.

Instead, *Business Beyond the Box* provides you with eight proven, everyday thinking strategies to get the most out of your cranial computer and achieve step-change, breakthrough business results. These are software programs for your cranial computer.

The strategies can be deployed like pyramid selling. Announce them to your immediate team, subordinates or contacts one a day this week; get them to do the same to their subordinates next week. Pretty soon the strategies are being widely used.

Incrementalism is supported by several specific habits and practices. Step-change, breakthrough results come from different, corresponding habits. If we are to go beyond the box and win, we'll need to weaken each of the habits supporting incrementalism and replace them with habits that generate breakthrough.

The key habits of incrementalism and step-change are as follows:

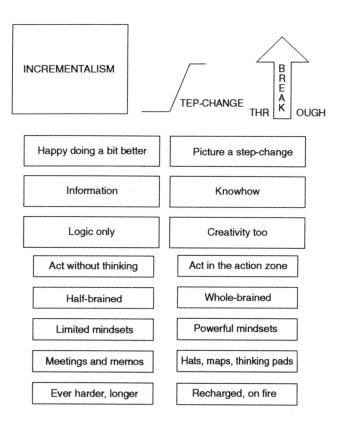

Happy doing a bit better	Picture a step-change
Information	Knowhow
Logic only	Creativity too
Act without thinking	Act in the action zone
Half-brained	Whole-brained
Limited mindsets	Powerful mindsets
Meetings and memos	Hats, maps, thinking pads
Ever harder, longer	Recharged, on fire

Changing each habit to the one that supports step-change rather than the one that supports incrementalism leads to the eight thinking strategies. In this book, we allocate a chapter to each strategy:

The eight thinking strategies

Picture a step-change	vs	Happy doing a bit better
Build knowhow	vs	Drown in information
Use creative thinking	vs	Logic alone
Act in the action zone	vs	Act without thinking
Become a whole-brained	vs	Half-brained organization
Choose powerful	vs	Limited mindsets
Hats, maps and thinking pads	vs	Meetings and memos
Recharge yourself, get on fire	vs	Ever harder, longer

The eight strategies form an 'arrow of breakthrough'. The first three form the arrowhead and the next five form the strands of the shaft.

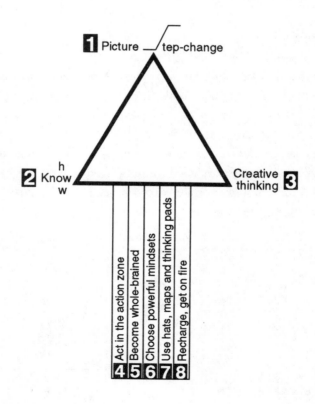

The arrowhead needs to have three sharp points to be effective; two only won't work. It is the first three strategies, working synergistically, which produce the power for breakthrough. At the same time, an arrowhead on its own isn't enough and you need a good strong shaft, provided by the other five strategies.

Tri△ngular thinking

The arrowhead is the key part of the arrow, without which it won't break through. The three points of the arrowhead are the key to great results and together form a concept of tri△ngular thinking. They refer to a focus on three things:

➤ Step-change goals
➤ Knowhow
➤ Creative thinking.

These should not be viewed as separate, independent activities, but as three elements of tri△ngular thinking that work together to get a significantly better result than any one alone. Remove any one of the three and you may do well, but you won't achieve breakthrough results.

As an analogy, view the elements of tri△ngular thinking in the same way as the three elements needed for fire – oxygen, fuel and heat. One on its own isn't enough, nor are two: you need all three. Take any one away and you put the fire out.

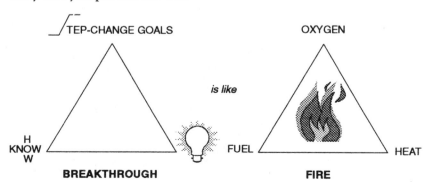

It's the same with breakthrough results. You need all three elements of triΔngular thinking together to go beyond the box: picturing a step-change, building knowhow and using creative thinking.

Too many individuals and organizations try to get breakthrough results by using only one of these elements at any time.

A focus on **step-change goals** alone isn't enough. It may cause the organization to feel stretched and stressed — and it is probably already stretched and stressed enough through the downsizing of the 1990s and the pace of change. Alternatively, the goals may be left as pipedreams. Either way, a focus on step-change goals alone isn't sufficient to generate great action steps and results.

A focus on **knowhow** alone also doesn't work. This leads to organizations becoming like universities. Too many will follow the 'learning organization' out of the window and spend too much time and effort, particularly in staff functions, developing knowledge that isn't really focused on getting results but on knowledge for its own sake. Indeed, in many organizations this will be used inappropriately to justify the importance, or even the existence, of particular departments.

Similarly, a focus on **creative thinking** alone doesn't work. It becomes sideshow entertainment rather than mainstream business. It becomes thought of only as brainstorming, creativity courses or off-site seances that aren't linked to the real world of business.

Step-change goals alone = Pipedream
Knowledge alone = University
Creative thinking alone = Entertainment

The secret is to focus on these three elements **together**: picturing step-change goals; searching for and building the specific knowledge that will help; and using creative thinking to generate action steps to hit those goals.

It is easy to get creative thinking from those with no knowledge, the young and inexperienced ones in the organization. But these ideas tend to go nowhere because of that very lack of knowledge.

Similarly, it is easy to get those with knowledge thinking only logically. That is the way most middle managers attempt to maintain the status quo, and it will result in incrementalism at best.

The beginnings of business beyond the box come when you get people with knowledge thinking creatively. That is the start of powerful action steps.

It also begins to solve the problem that most organizations face of striking a balance between keeping managers continually in a job to develop expertise and knowledge and making a change, even if the newcomer has no knowledge, in order to get the benefit of a fresh mindset. Being able to get fresh mindsets in people who already have expertise and knowledge is likely to yield the potential for breakthrough results.

Easy, weak	People with no knowledge, thinking creatively
Easy, weak	People with knowledge, thinking only logically
Breakthrough	People with knowledge, thinking creatively, towards a big step-change goal

This approach to achieving breakthrough results forms **tri△ngular thinking**.

Several years ago, Edward de Bono moved us on from vertical thinking to lateral thinking. Tri△ngular thinking is the next stage.

Vertical thinking has always had the limitation of seeming 'tunnel-visioned', of keeping our thinking in a restricted channel that was likely at best to bring incremental improvements, but not breakthrough.

Lateral thinking moved us on from the restrictions of vertical thinking. It got us 'out of the box', and helped us think 'differently'. It helped us invent and consider new options to solve problems. And occasionally, by great happenstance, it helped produce breakthrough results when we happened to hit on a piece of lateral thinking that 'worked'.

However, there have been several limitations in putting lateral thinking to work in the business environment. It has often seemed directionless. Lateral can mean go anywhere, and often did. Sometimes people got it mixed up with 'the crazier the better'. Lateral is often interpreted as simply 'avoidance of vertical' and can end up in loose ideas that aren't usable.

Tri△ngular thinking helps overcome this. By starting out with 'picturing step-change', the thinking process has a real focus and direction.

By insisting on building knowhow at the same time, there is a very good chance that the action steps and ideas you come up with will be practical and usable.

The three arrowhead strategies

The first three arrowhead strategies can be divided into two alternative thinking systems that will generate completely different action steps and results. On the one side are the three elements we are aiming for, which form a system to achieve breakthrough results. On the other side there are the three things that keep you in the box of incrementalism – happy doing a bit better; using selective information to reinforce it; and using unremitting logic alone to justify it and explain why doing anything more is completely unrealistic.

Breakthrough	**Incrementalism**
Picture a step-change	Happy doing a bit better
Build knowhow	Drown in information
Use creative thinking	Logic alone

An example in action

Consider a global brand which is sold in many different countries. Take one particular country in which the brand is growing and its market share for the last three years has been 8 percent, 9 percent and 10 percent. What should be its share target for next year?

Incrementalism

Under the system of incrementalism, the country organization would probably think of 11 percent share as next year's achievement. With that in mind, they might even suggest something slightly lower for the budget target, say 10.5 percent, in order to promise something they are pretty sure they could achieve. After all, they would say, success is achieving your targets, so negotiating for a 10.5 percent target makes sense.

The individual and organization would then seek selective information to help justify why that target is right. They would find some things that helped the brand in the base period that won't be available next year. They would also select information on some things that are likely to happen next year, such as predicted competitive activity, that make continued growth more difficult.

They would then use unremitting logic to justify why 10.5 percent is the right share target. And they would use logic alone to come up with some sort of action steps to achieve it, similar to those that have been in place before.

If challenged to do better, say to aim for 11 percent, the incremental organization would defend the 10.5 percent and focus on all the logical reasons why doing better was just not possible next year. The whole organization's energies and thought processes will be focused on a range of achievement next year between 0.5 percent and 11 percent, compared to 10 percent this year.

Tri△ngular thinking for breakthrough results

Under this approach, the country organization would not look back at its own history for a target for next year. It would look outwards at other countries in which the brand is sold and ask: 'What is the highest market share achieved anywhere else in the world on this brand?' It would probably find countries with over a 30 percent market share.

Managers would then seek to find out how that country got its 30 percent share. What exactly did the organization there do? They would 'go to the horse's mouth', to people who were actually in the business at the time of building the 30 percent share, to get their knowhow. They would not just restrict themselves to asking questions of the current position holders. They would then use creative thinking to reapply what they had learnt, adapt it as necessary for their situation and also come up with creative ideas for getting their own business to a 30 percent share. They may not all be practical and they may take time to work, but this approach will result in the organization considering substantial changes.

These two thinking systems are distinctly different and will produce different action steps – and different results.

How high is the bar?

A very simple model can be used to understand the tri∆ngular thinking system for breakthrough results using the three key arrowhead strategies. Moreover, it is memorable and fun and can help transmit the idea to others.

Looking at the picture below, how would an individual, or an organization, normally decide how high to set the bar?

The first question is logical and seeks the information: 'How high did I clear last time?' Based on that, you would set the bar just a little bit higher.

You would then try to get over the slightly higher height. If you succeed, you will feel very good indeed. You've jumped higher than you ever have before: a personal best to celebrate.

You would then repeat the process and try for a slightly higher height. If you succeed, you again feel very good. You've set a new personal record.

Using this system, you could achieve record results. Indeed, as a minimum, you might even achieve the world record by a person of your surname, of your age, jumping on Thursdays.

Now consider a different picture:

Take a few minutes to consider how you would get over the second bar. Don't read on until you've spent a minute thinking about it. There is no one right answer but lots of possible answers. Say out loud to yourself the ideas you come up with. Try and think of half a dozen or more now.

Key learning

This simple exercise illustrates the central mechanism of the three elements of triΔngular thinking working together: picturing a step-change, building knowhow and using creative thinking.

First, when picturing a step-change height, the brain automatically – in a nano-second – switches off thoughts of incrementalism. It immediately realizes that it will never get over this height by pursuing the incremental approach of the high-jump. Incrementalism will not work: the brain has to move to a new Website.

Secondly, to reach a solution the brain scans for knowledge about other systems that get this high. Many people quickly find the pole vault, which is not very far away, in the same athletics area. Such scanning turns up things like a trampoline or a ladder. And that triggers knowledge of similar systems like the mobile staircase for going up to an airplane. Scanning your knowledge produces the knowhow to solve this particular problem. And the brain focuses on building this knowhow and ignores all the information about incremental high-jump performances.

Thirdly, the brain also takes some of the underlying principles and starts inventing creative ways of getting over the step-change height: spring-heeled shoes, flying over, jet-propelled backpacks, using a helicopter and the like; even cutting the poles to bring the bar down to a height you can jump over.

All three elements of triΔngular thinking are important. The brain uses them naturally. You can supercharge the natural workings of your brain by focusing on the strategies of picturing step-change, building knowhow and using creative thinking, to come up with action steps to hit those breakthrough goals.

The exercise also draws out the two different thinking systems of the box of incrementalism and the system for step-change, breakthrough results. They are two distinct systems and you can choose which one you want to operate in at any one time.

There will still be many places where the incremental system is vital – checking progress on immediate results, solving today's crises, making sure this year's budgets or this quarter's results are on track. If you want breakthough results, however, you'll need a different approach. And on any issue or business area you can decide how much of your time you want to spend on incremental thinking and how much on breakthrough or step-change.

You can switch from one to the other: you decide when you do so.

The results

The results from the two systems will be very different. At best, on the incremental system you will achieve a slightly better height than last time. Eventually, you will be reduced to aiming for very, very small improvements. You'll finally get stuck at a particular height – stuck in the box of incrementalism.

The triΔngular thinking system for breakthrough achieves far, far bigger heights. Each and every method you imagined, created or adapted from knowhow will achieve breakthrough heights compared to the incrementalism of the high-jump method.

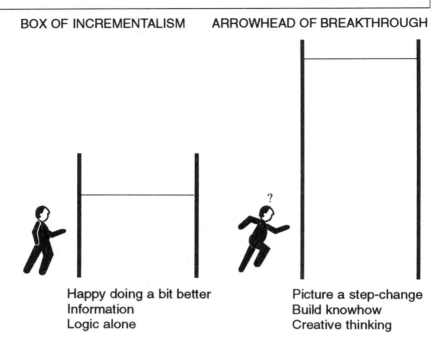

BOX OF INCREMENTALISM   ARROWHEAD OF BREAKTHROUGH

Happy doing a bit better   Picture a step-change
Information   Build knowhow
Logic alone   Creative thinking

The shaft of the arrow

An arrowhead alone is not enough. It needs the support of a shaft. The next five strategies form the strands of the shaft.

Act in the action zone versus act without thinking addresses the need to take action. Many people will become impatient with any thinking strategy unless it results in action, or if it delays action too much. This issue needs to be tackled up front, or else people lose interest in thinking. This thinking strategy gives a way to handle both thinking and action.

Become a whole-brained versus a half-brained organization is a strategy designed to maximize the power of your thinking, with whatever strategy you are working. Many people are only left-brained in their thinking, trying to use reasoning alone. This is half-brained. There is terrific power to be had in adding right-brained imagination and gut feeling to left-brained reasoning. Breakthrough results will be helped by the strategy of choosing to be whole-brained rather than half-brained.

Similarly, results will be helped by the next thinking strategy in the shaft: **choose powerful versus limited mindsets.** We all have mindsets, it's inevitable. So the only sensible strategy, if you want to get breakthrough results, is to decide to adopt powerful mindsets rather than allowing yourself to pick up or continue with limited ones.

The next shaft strategy addresses the fact that most people continue the habits of **meetings and memos** almost without thinking. Yet about 80 percent of our time and thinking energy are absorbed in these. To get breakthrough results, adopt a strategy of using **mindmaps, thinking hats and thinking pads**, instead of meetings and memos.

The final strand of the shaft is to choose the strategy of **recharging yourself and getting on fire** versus the alternative of continuing with an assumption that ever longer, ever harder is best.

Breakthrough results will be facilitated by making the positive choices suggested in each of the shaft strategies in preference to the alternatives.

Operating principles beyond the box

In this book there is a chapter on each of the strategies to help move individuals and organizations out of the box of incrementalism and towards the thinking systems that will bring breakthrough results.

As you work with each of these strategies, do so with two operating principles in mind that will make them very powerful.

1 Use push as well as pull
2 Use the heart as well as the head

Use push as well as pull

Too many individuals and organizations think that they will generate powerful action because of the pull of the choice of what you want to move towards; that provision of a vision is enough; that it is the anticipated pleasure of the carrot which stimulates action.

However, powerful action doesn't just come from the anticipation of pleasure – it also comes from the avoidance of pain. As much action comes from avoiding the pain of the crippling stick as from wanting to achieve the pleasure of the juicy carrot. The power of push and pull together is enormous:

Pull	*and*	**Push**
Vision		Dissatisfaction with the status quo
Move towards something		Something to avoid
Attraction of pleasure		Avoidance of pain
Juicy carrot		Crippling stick

Breakthrough results occur when both factors are present.

Great results can come from the addition of 'push' to 'pull'. For example, in a crisis an individual or organization can perform dramatic feats. A crisis, by definition, dictates that the status quo is unacceptable – it just won't produce the needed results.

Many individuals and organizations achieve terrific performance in a crisis, then slip back to a comfortable business-as-usual afterwards. The key to step-change results is to retain the underlying forces of a crisis when the crisis is over. This means making the current situation untenable, as well as making a different future attractive.

➤ It is as important to get hugely dissatisfied with the status quo and the box of incrementalism as it is to get motivated by the attraction of breakthrough results.

➤ It is as important to get dissatisfied with drowning in information pollution as it is to get motivated by seeking knowhow that helps.

➤ It is as important to get hugely dissatisfied with logic-only thinking as it is to get motivated by thinking creatively.

The same principle applies to each strategy.

Use the heart as well as the head

The most power, the most action, the most energy from any thinking strategy will come if you can put your heart into it as well as your head. And if you can make it appeal to other people's hearts as well as their heads. They will do far greater things if they have passion and inspiration – rather than being merely intellectually in agreement.

Whole-brained activity is dealt with in detail in Chapter 7. But the essential learning is that the power of the brain is huge when both halves – the logical left half and the emotional right half – are used synergistically. The power from the whole brain is not just double the power from using either half. It's more like fifty or a hundred times.

You can engage the right half of the brain with images, metaphors and pictures that inspire. This is what happens in rousing speeches or motivational sales meetings. Put differently, power will come from using the 'sales meeting culture' as well as the 'financial report culture'.

Head	*and*	**Heart**
Logic		Passion
Analysis		Emotion
Facts		Imagination
Financial report culture		Sales meeting culture
Intellectual agreement		Fired-up commitment

Remember these two operating principles – push as well as pull, heart as well as head – as we consider each strategy in turn. For each strategy, you need a focus on what you want to move towards *and* energy around the alternative you want to move away from. Get fired up about achieving the elements to bring breakthrough and emotionally committed to avoiding the elements that will leave you in the box of incrementalism.

The First
Thinking Strategy

Picture a

step-change

versus

Be happy doing a bit better

3 Picturing a Step-Change

Relying primarily on a Kaizen philosophy will yield 'me-too' products and processes, 'let's-play-it-safe' strategies, and a 'we're-no-worse-than-anyone-else mind-set', any of which will very likely prove fatal in today's whitewater environment.

Toyota

The best way to get step-change, breakthrough **results** is to start by picturing a step-change, breakthrough **objective**. There will be a difference in the action steps you come up with if you and the organization are aiming for breakthrough, instead of just aiming to do a little better than before.

Think big: whoever heard of Alexander the Average?

Imagine you are running a brand that has a static 10 percent market share and there is a big product improvement coming up. On the one hand, if you develop a mindset that the product change is likely to improve the share to about 12 percent then you will develop ideas and plans that will result in that. These will involve marketing plans that are stronger than previous ones, but not necessarily radically different. And you may achieve the 12 percent share, or perhaps 11 percent.

By contrast, if you picture using the product change to double your share, from 10 percent to 20 percent, you would generate very different action steps. You would consider ways to double or triple the distribution of the product; double or triple the marketing budget; double the advertising; perhaps do broad sampling; and then you'd consider how to pay for it all, perhaps by having a higher price justified by the better product.

As we've seen, if you do set out just for incremental improvement, then you'll generate only the sort of action steps that will achieve that, and only that. Logical incrementalism – 'happy doing a bit better' – is prevalent in most bureaucracies and middle- to low-performing organizations. You do not need much imagination, or knowledge, to achieve this, and the full potential of the organization is often unfulfilled.

The sorts of action steps an organization comes up with, the sorts of knowledge it seeks, the sorts of thinking it uses, are directly related to the size of the goal pictured in people's heads.

The concept behind this thinking strategy is consistent with much current management theory and practice.

The idea of big goals, called stretch goals, is alive and well at General Electric. CEO Jack Welch has made a name for himself with them. If you look at what GE executives have said about stretch goals, the principles are completely in line with the principles advocated in this book:

> ➤ *There's plenty of evidence that if you don't find dramatically new ways of doing business, you are not going to be in business. And if you don't intrude artificially into what's going on, you probably won't come up with radical out-of-the-box ideas. So clearly some intervention is needed.*

➤ *It's not the number per se, especially because it's a made-up number. It's rather the process you're trying to stimulate. You're trying to get people to think of fundamentally better ways of performing their work, to cut out unnecessary work.*

➤ *Stretch targets are an artificial stimulant for finding ways to work more efficiently. They force you to think 'out-of-the-box'.*

➤ *It's popular today for companies to ask their people to double sales, or increase speed to market three-fold. But then they don't provide their people with the knowledge, tools, and means to meet such ambitious goals.*

This last quote reinforces the concept of tri△ngular thinking and the arrowhead of breakthrough. It's not enough just to consider step-change goals; that's good, but it isn't enough. You need also to build knowhow to help achieve the goals and give people the creative thinking tools to help devise new methods.

In late 1997, the *Harvard Business Review* carried an interview with John Browne, head of British Petroleum. BP has transformed itself in a decade and is now the most profitable of the major oil companies.

It believes in breakthrough thinking. Browne's approach, in the context of developing economically an oilfield called Andrew, was described as follows:

> *He saw the opportunity to demonstrate the power of breakthrough thinking. The approach: set a seemingly unattainable target and see how close you can get to attaining it by assigning the best minds to the problem, scouring the world for the best ideas – doing whatever it takes.*

Once again, this reinforces the concept of tri△ngular thinking around the arrowhead of breakthrough: picture a step-change, build knowhow, use creative thinking.

John Browne also added:

> *The conventional wisdom is that excelling in incremental learning is a science – a matter of installing the right processes – while excelling in breakthrough thinking is more of an art. I disagree about the latter. I think you can install processes that generate breakthrough thinking. We have.*

So there are good examples from management practice to reinforce these thinking strategies to achieve breakthrough results. In particular they stress the importance of picturing step-change and of setting stretch or discontinuous goals.

Increasingly, there are also examples reinforcing the need to move away from incrementalism, as well as moving towards step-change.

For example, Nokia, the hugely successful Swedish mobile phone company, identifies and then attacks a concept of 'NOYRYYS', a Scandinavian term referring to complacency. It insists on 'no mediocracy'.

Or as Toyota admits: 'Kaizen is not enough'. And Michael Hammer reminds us that nowadays: 'If you think you're good, you're dead.'

Really breakthrough results – in line with the operating principle of both push and pull – will come when we are fired up at picturing step-change and highly dissatisfied with logical incrementalism. Both halves of the strategy are key and this chapter will provide tips and techniques to do both.

There are certain situations when it's relatively easy to see that logical incrementalism is unacceptable and the organization takes drastic action. For example:

➤ **There is a crisis**. By definition, a crisis dictates that 'being happy doing a bit better' is no good. The crisis means that something different needs to be done. It's amazing that when the factory burns down the replacement is often built in half the time it would take to build the equivalent-size factory as a capacity expansion.

➤ **The business is losing money heavily**. Then vigorous action is taken to change things. Logical incrementalism won't do; drastic action is indicated. In fact, it's often easier to get from losing $10 million to break even than it is subsequently to get from break even to making $5 million profit. This is because the organization can get fired up about eliminating losses but then reverts to incremental approaches to building profits subsequently.

➤ **Building a business from scratch or expanding to new territory**. Being happy doing a bit better is clearly not challenging enough. Far more vigorous action is often taken to build a business than is taken to improve an existing one.

➤ **Your predecessor made a mess of it.** Again, it is transparent that small changes are not enough, and massive change takes place. Bigger change is easier than if your predecessor had been considered a great success.

➤ **Sales progress** is like this:
Massive action ensues because 'being happy doing a bit better' is clearly unacceptable.

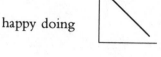

In all the above situations, individuals and organizations can produce big actions to make a significant change in results. Clearly, dissatisfaction with the status quo is a powerful force. However, it's easy to create change when the business is failing. It's more difficult – but just as valuable – to generate it when 'business as usual' seems acceptable. This is a key ability to master to achieve breakthrough results. Later we'll cover tips and techniques to help do this.

But first, are you sure your heart is really in it? Are you really committed to achieving step-change and being dissatisfied with incrementalism? Do you really, really want it? There is no point in going further if you don't, because if your heart isn't in it you will fail.

Head and heart

Are you using both your heart and your head to become attracted by the pleasure of thinking big *and* fed up with being happy only doing a little bit better? How do you do this?

➤ How do you get yourself addicted to the thrill of picturing step-change objectives, fired up by the adrenaline of realizing we can all aim at BIG things and refusing to waste our talent, our time, our lives on anything else?

➤ How do you get yourself deeply demoralized by being stuck in the box of incrementalism, working only at fairly trivial improvements to your life and work and living out a humdrum existence of continuing with the status quo?

Here are some emotional thoughts that may help to drive some passion.

Getting demoralized by incrementalism

It takes as much effort and energy to work at a boring, mundane improvement to any part of our work and lives – which any one of a hundred people could have done – as it does to deploy our minds and talent trying to do something substantially more meaningful. The problem is that we never take five minutes out to realize this.

➤ How often do we become involved in relatively petty arguments about relatively petty things? Why not put all that energy and commitment into going after something worthwhile?

➤ How often do we just get stuck in a rut, without realizing it, believing that a minor improvement on where we are is a cause for celebration?

➤ How often do we, almost subconsciously, accept the status quo and happily work within it?

➤ Are we living or are we dying? Will there be anything to write on our gravestone that makes us any more distinctive, memorable or contributing more than millions of others living this very minute? Are we destined simply to come into the world, perhaps mate with another and spend our lives going through the humdrum activity of producing and raising two new humans to replace the two mates? Talk about going round in circles.

➤ At work, are we simply to live out a commonplace existence, going for mediocre improvements, just like millions of others in hundreds of other corporations, all in their own little boxes just like us, earning a wage to keep us alive until we're dead?

➤ Next month, even if it is March, starts a new year. March to next February. Is there any real point in us living that year or might we just as well go into a coma? Are we merely going to aim for this year being a little bit better than last year – and accept it if it's not? Will the world be any different for us having lived this year? Will we ourselves be any different, for the better, after the year is over?

➤ How about next month, or next week? Are we really aiming to make a big difference – or are we just continuing to exist as before, perhaps a little better, stuck in the box of incrementalism, imprisoned by old habits and routines, without knowing it, concentrated on the scraps of work and life?

➤ If we were seen from Mars, wouldn't we be just like one ant in a colony of ants at our feet in a wood – focused on things that to us are minutia and trivia? You live in a box called a house – is it really so different from all the other boxes? You travel in a box on wheels – is it really so different from all the other boxes? You go to an office block to work in a cubbyhole – is it really so different from all the other blocks? And when we make minor improvements to our boxes, we're still in the box of incrementalism.

➤ Are you dressed in a box called a suit, perhaps the same color as all the other boxes, with perhaps an incremental difference of a wider stripe, or perhaps choosing a slightly different tie or a brightly colored blouse – an incremental difference that you celebrate as a major distinctiveness?

➤ Is what you do during a work day really just existing in a box of routines and habits established by others before you or around you – celebrating incremental changes or improvements as being significant?

➤ Are things really, in the big scheme of things, going to be that much better for you acting out your life this day, this week, this month, this year?

➤ Do you want to stay stuck in a rut? Accepting your state in life? Accepting where you are, what you have, what you do as being 'given' and looking at a modest change or improvement you make as being a cause for celebration?

➤ Whatever job you do, whatever role you play, whatever life you lead, you can aim for step-change results within that job, that role, that life, rather than being content with just making it marginally better.

Has the above made you feel bad? Has it made you upset, discontented with being in a box? If so, great, because it has generated passion and power. If it hasn't made you thoroughly dissatisfied, read it again.

Getting addicted to seeking step-change

There is another way of looking at things. Remember, you are an absolutely unique person. Never in the whole history of humankind has there been anybody exactly like you, who looks like you, sounds like you. You are a unique combination of chromosomes inherited from your particular parents in a particular way that is you. Even if your parents had 50 children, not one of these children would be exactly like you.

When you walk down the street, how many people do you see who look even remotely like you, let alone come close to your unique set of experiences, knowledge, attitudes, personality traits and skills?

And your individual talent and ability are hugely underused, as are everyone's. You actively employ only about 5 percent of the brain-power you have. You know you have periods of super-high energy and attitude – when things just fly – but you get into this state less than 5 percent of the time. You are brilliant in a crisis, but the other 95 percent of the time you relax back to a mind-numbing routine.

The energy and mindpower and time it takes to work for a small incremental improvement could just as easily be used in working for the kind of discontinuous improvement of which you are fully capable.

You can spend your day on small things. Or you can spend your day on BIG things. You can fuss about petty things, get upset at small issues, or you can focus your energy on something really worthwhile.

So it must be better to spend your time on things you can be proud of – achievements that you could tell strangers about, that would not seem incremental and mundane, but big and special. Achievements that are worthy of your life energies and life time.

Get addicted to working for step-change. Nothing else is worth your time or talent. There is only a point in putting your time and energy into something if you are going to aim to make a step-change difference.

Get depressed and demoralized about working merely at incremental changes. They are trivial, not worthy of your time.

Don't leave this chapter until step-change is all you want to do, an addiction, a habit, and you won't drift into aiming just for incrementalism on anything.

> Some men die in shrapnel
> Some go down in flames
> Most men perish inch by inch
> Playing little games

And use the techniques described above to get others in your organization depressed and demoralized about working on incrementalism and addicted to picturing step-change, breakthrough results.

A *personal case history*

In the mid-1980s, I took over as managing director of Procter & Gamble's UK subsidiary, after spending most of my career away from the UK. The UK was the biggest P&G subsidiary outside of the US and the most successful. Compared to other international subsidiaries, it had at the time some of the best brand shares, the best profit margins, and felt it produced some of the best managers.

The organization was doing well. More importantly, it was happy continually to be doing better. Each year was somewhat better than the year before. People were rightly being promoted as a result.

Yet to someone who had spent the previous 13 years operating in businesses around the world, the full potential of the business wasn't being realized. On average the results were good, and much better than the UK's history, but many of the individual brands were not operating to their fullest potential – and not to the same level achieved on similar brands elsewhere. If a brand had a 25 percent leading share in the UK why couldn't that be 35 percent or 40 percent – as I had experienced in other markets? If a profit margin was good at 15 percent, why not achieve 25 percent? And why accept that any brand in the portfolio was doing poorly?

Overall, the total profits were considered very good, and improving by 10 percent or so each year. And that was seen as a cause for celebration – particularly when compared with a very deep and troubled history when the business hadn't been making any money at all, which many of the business managers could remember.

However, rather than being happy to be doing better, I persuaded the organization to set a step-change goal – well ahead of the then budgeted forecasts. What could we do if we were all that we could be? What could we aim for if we didn't have to promise it in the budget?

Instead of growing profits at 10 percent a year, we decided that the potential was to **double within three years**. Setting and committing to such a step-change goal produced significantly different actions. Instead of considering, and being satisfied with, overall good results, the organization became dissatisfied with any part of the business that wasn't all that it could be.

Any brand losing money was called a 'bleeder' and bleeding had to be stopped. This was in contrast to considering it an investment for the future even when it really wasn't and there was just a vague hope of bringing it into profit in a few years' time. Bleeding was unacceptable and had to be stopped now. And we made that emotional as well as logical.

Even a brand doing well overall had some variants or sizes that were losing money. This had been accepted for a variety of historical reasons. But under a step-change goal of doubling the profit, no bleeding on any part of a brand was acceptable.

Investments were focused on healthy, buoyant brands with good market shares, and on building these market shares to levels achieved elsewhere in similar categories. All the fuel was focused on these 'rockets' to get big profitable growth. Rocket is a positive, emotional term.

Brands that were meant to be harvested were turned into 'little goldmines', rather than celebrating only modest harvests. Problem brands, or variants, were subjected to 'kill or cure'. These phrases engaged the heart as well as the head.

The organization moved to an attitude that not all marketing spending was considered of equal quality. Each brand had to justify its support on the basis of the quality of the investment, not based on previous years' base levels. We took the mindset that much of our spending was poor quality – and set out to identify and eliminate 'wasted' spending. We put half of the savings back to reinforce programs that worked well and took half to the bottom line. The term 'wasted' combines logic with emotion.

Margins on leading brands were stretched to levels achieved on similar brands elsewhere in the world – in contrast to being satisfied with incremental improvements over previous years. Acceptable margins were demanded on each and every variant and size, rather than accepting the traditional explanations as to why a particular item would have to be underperforming.

The overall result was a transformation of profitability. Instead of continuing the pattern of 10 percent per year growth, off a good base, profit was doubled in about two and a half years.

This is a clear example of the benefits of setting step-change goals versus being happy to be doing better.

Key tips and techniques

What are the key tips and techniques for getting dissatisfied with the status quo of logical incrementalism *and* getting fired up by picturing step-change?

Five tips for avoiding logical incrementalism

1 Face up to the rate of change: look forward not backward
2 Measure the degree of healthy dissatisfaction
3 Graph out incrementalism
4 Compare with the worst not the best
5 Use emotional strategies

Face up to the rate of change: look forward not backward

People have a tendency to escape into the comfortable past and into an assumption that things can carry on as they always have. This allows us to feel that business as usual is acceptable.

In fact, in most situations, we have our heads in the sand. We are ducking the issue of the rate of change around us, because we don't want to face up to it. We have almost 'retired on the job'. We take solace in concepts like: 'It's served us very well for a number of years, why change?'

However, when we look at the horizon rather than at history, it is not just easy to become dissatisfied with 'business as usual', we become frightened by the degree of change needed to adjust to the future.

The rate of change around us is so fast that it is clear there will be a gap between where our business is going and where the world about us will be.

Look forward to the future – to changes that will happen – and you will quickly realize that logical incrementalism from where you have been will not bring you breakthrough results in the world you're heading to.

Consider advertisements selling mutual funds or unit trusts that celebrate their great performance track record, possibly comparing it favorably with competitors. In many countries, the authorities force them to put a warning on the advertisement: 'Historical performance is no guide to future prospects.'

So look forward on your own operation. It must be clear that as a minimum, information systems, the Internet and rapidly changing technology will all have an effect on you one way or another, let alone the more specific, down-to-earth changes you can see before your very eyes if only you open them.

Measure the degree of healthy dissatisfaction

Many individuals and organizations state that they encourage a healthy dissatisfaction with the status quo. But few examine whether they really have it.

For example, ask a group of managers: 'Hands up, who has a healthy dissatisfaction with the status quo?' Many would put their hands up. Now ask them to imagine that tomorrow they were going to take over their neighbor's job and their neighbor was going to take over their job. In other words, tomorrow everybody in the organization is going to change jobs.

Would the level of dissatisfaction with the status quo be higher or lower than it is today? Most would say substantially higher. Yet if today we think we have a healthy level, is it today's level that is right and optimum, or is it the level we could get tomorrow by changing people in their jobs?

The point is that we don't spend enough time thinking about what is the right level of healthy dissatisfaction and whether we have achieved it. We tend simply to assume that the degree of dissatisfaction we're feeling at any particular time is the right level.

Contrast this with how much time we spend thinking and debating about whether we have the right objectives and goals to aim for. We consider them in detail, put numbers to them, reconcile them and so on.

Yet if massive action is triggered by the combination of the attraction of the goal you want to aim for and the dissatisfaction with what you want to move away from, then our thinking time is spent too much in the former and not enough in the latter. The indicated action is:

> Split your thinking time between:
> How to get the right goals to aim for.
> How to get the right dissatisfaction with
> the status quo.

Graph out incrementalism

Incrementalism is fueled by numerical calculations of percentages and indices. Consider a business whose share has grown over the last three years from 8 percent to 9 percent to 10 percent to 11 percent. On the one hand, very good. But plot out the results over the whole history of the business and they may look like this over the last 12 years:

Market share result, %

Yr	1	2	3	4	5	6	7	8	9	10	11	12
	8	9	9	8	7	9	8	7	8	9	10	11

By looking at 'growth versus previous year' there might appear to be some big changes year to year. And the most recent four years look good in comparison to the pattern of previous years.

But looking at it in overview, the business has always had about a 9 percent share and no really dramatic change has been made.

To illustrate this, instead of calculating '% growth versus previous year', graph out the results over time, using an insensitive vertical axis that has zero market share as its base and 100 percent market share at the top. Incrementalism then becomes transparent. This is a line of incrementalism at around a 9 percent market share.

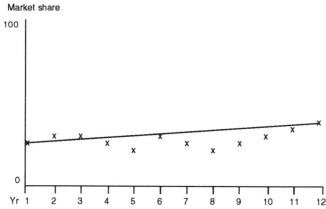

Instead of a line of incrementalism, aim to have a line of step-change as in the graph below.

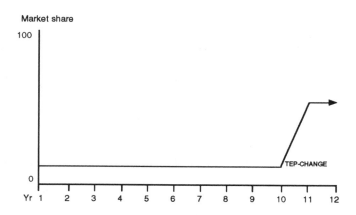

Graph your own organization's results over the last few years on an insensitive axis and get dissatisfied with your incrementalism.

Compare with the worst not the best

Comparing with the best is a popular technique. It has a lot of power if your own performance is truly awful. However, in many cases this is not the best system to trigger massive action.

Too many individuals and organizations use a weak approach for generating action, in whatever sphere or activity they are considering:

Weak approach
A Describe the best system
B Identify how good you are versus it
C Aim to bridge the gap

This is a weak approach because people tend to overrate how good they are in comparison. They search for the good points and gloss over the bad ones. Moreover, the assessment is often that you are 70 or 80 percent as good as the best. That doesn't generate dissatisfaction. It's quite a high number in absolute and 'acceptable' at face value. After all, if all our examination marks were at this level in every subject, we'd be very pleased.

A common situation where this arises is in measuring 'customer delivery service' or 'perfect order processing'. Most systems produce answers like: 'Our customer delivery service was 98.1 percent', i.e. 98.1 percent of deliveries were made at the scheduled time. This is a big number and doesn't drive discontent. The same applies to: '97.2 percent of our orders were processed perfectly.' That seems pretty good. However, it doesn't seem so good when you quote the numbers the other way round – 1.9 percent of deliveries were late: exactly how many physical deliveries is that? 2.8 percent of orders were mishandled: how many orders is that in absolute? This drives different dissatisfaction and action.

A more powerful approach is to do the opposite to 'the best system' approach:

Powerful approach

A   Describe the worst possible system you can imagine
B   Identify if any element of your current situation is like this
C   Get hugely dissatisfied

This generates significantly more, healthy dissatisfaction. For example, rather than being complacent that your team meetings are becoming more effective, describe the behavior of the worst sort of team meeting and see if you exhibit this at all. Then get hugely dissatisfied with the waste of your talent and aim for a real step-change in effectiveness.

Use emotional strategies

As well as the logical strategies of facing up to the rate of change, graphing out incrementalism and comparing with the worst, feel free to act on emotional strategies to generate dissatisfaction. Display the 'Some men fall in shrapnel' poem. Generate other sayings such as:

'Afflict the comfortable' rather than 'comfort the afflicted'.
Make comfort zones into discomfort zones.

Emotional strategies can be hugely powerful when combined with logical ones to generate dissatisfaction.

Consider most top sports performers: when interviewed after a performance that the interviewer thinks was splendid, many of them disagree rather than agree. They don't want to make themselves complacent. They find something in their performance to get intensely dissatisfied about and then 'complain' about how bad that part of their game was, in a downbeat way. They know that is what is required to give them the energy and fire to go out and practice incessantly. It's not enough to have the vision of a victory, they need to get emotionally dissatisfied with where they are. By contrast, the 'normal' person after a good performance focuses on remembering the good parts and goes off to have a drink to celebrate.

So use emotional strategies as well as logical ones to generate dissatisfaction with the status quo.

These are techniques for getting dissatisfied with the status quo. What are the techniques to get fired up through picturing a step-change?

Ten tips to help picture step-change

1 Reach for the stars
2 Separate step-change from the budget promise
3 Draw word pictures of step-change
4 Hire the world's four best thinkers
5 Your personal talents deserve more
6 Don't dream vaguely and dread precisely: dream precisely and dread vaguely
7 Accept risk
8 Distinguish between a miss and a mistake
9 Dovetail coil-downs and harvests
10 Set step-change goals not stretch goals

Reach for the stars

Too many people and organizations measure themselves by whether or not they achieve the goals they set. Success becomes misdefined as 'achieving what you said you would' or 'delivering what you promised'. This leads to incremental results at best.

To achieve success in these terms, there is as much skill, time and thinking effort spent in lowering expectations and getting a softer target as there is in getting actual results. 'Aim low and overdeliver' ends up with only a modest improvement in absolute terms.

The alternative mindset that will generate breakthrough results is to measure success by the absolute achievement – not by how it compares with your promise.

When people are liberated by this approach, they set their sights higher. They aim for bigger changes that may not fully work but will move them forward more than repeating tired, traditional approaches.

'When you reach for the stars, you may
not quite get one, but you won't come
up with a handful of mud either.'
Leo Burnett

At any stage, at any business review, allow yourselves and others to announce a 'reach for the stars' period of discussion and effort – that recognizes that you and the team are deliberately aiming unrealistically high, in order to end up far higher than you otherwise would.

Separate step-change from the budget promise

This is the key issue in most organizations. On the one hand, people are happy to aim high. On the other hand, they fear that their bosses will take this and use it to stretch their forecast target or budget promise. And their performance is measured on meeting their forecast, target or budget. So people become unwilling to engage in 'thinking big' for fear that the resultant bigger numbers will be taken as an expectation of their performance.

The technique to solve this is to separate out the step-change, 'reach-for-the-stars' process from the budget process. Formally establish it as a separate exercise. One useful aid is to aim for step-change achievement in a calendar year, to keep it separate from budgets done on a fiscal year basis.

Additionally, split up business reviews and meetings between the two types of thinking processes, as illustrated by 'high-jump incrementalism' and 'pole-vault step-change'.

'High-jump incrementalism' is to do with the results and problems of the budget for this week, this month, this year. These results are important and action needs to be taken to ensure that current performance is going to be good enough.

'Pole-vault step-change' is to do with considering step-change goals and the kind of action that might be considered in this context. However, these sorts of actions might need to be tested before being implemented broadly; they may take longer to see results; they may involve accepting some short-term disruption, but would be accepted in a planned way in the context of aiming for a bigger goal.

Keep incremental adjustments to the budget separate from step-change thinking. Over time, this separation won't be so important, for two reasons:

➤ The new action steps will work. Every action step you thought of for getting over the higher bar worked. And each 'step-change' method got you over a higher height than incrementalism on the high jump would have done.

➤ You won't mind promising higher on the high jump if you have a pole in your back pocket to help you get over it.

Draw word pictures of step-change

Often an organization starts with a pattern of figures on historical results and then tries to set a step-change goal with a number alone:

				GOAL
93/94	94/95	95/96	96/97	99/00
103	107	110	113	130

This is a weak approach for two reasons. First, it forces the mind into the pattern of past results. It is conditioned by the past and the status quo. That's not the power you want. At today's rate of change, what on earth has what happened three years ago really got to do with the future you want to create in three years' time? Why should you let the latter be limited by the results of the former?

The second reason this is a weak approach is that a number alone doesn't engage the whole brain in describing a step-change. By contrast, the advantage of the 'picture' in the high-jump/pole-vault metaphor is that it gives something for the whole brain to engage in.

It engages more than the left brain, which deals with logic and numbers. It engages the right brain – where imagination for creativity and passion for power lie – through a picture.

Step-change goals work best when they are framed in a way that captures the right brain as well as the left. It is very difficult to picture the average number as a goal. It stays in the rational left side only. It often doesn't trigger anything. A sales target of 2240 cases doesn't trigger much. Nor does a market share target of 17.2 percent, or a target cost of £4.37. The only potential inspiration or relevance of these numbers could come from a year-by-year comparison with the achievements of the past, and that's exactly what you want to avoid.

Some 'round numbers' in word pictures are more magical, help drive whole-brain activity and are good for step-change goals:

➤ Double profit in two years
➤ Reach a million-dollar turnover
➤ Get to 50 percent market share
➤ Cut costs in half

Draw a word-picture, or use metaphors and analogies, to help describe what it would look like and so stimulate the imagination:

➤ Get 50 percent of the world's men to use this brand
➤ Make this brand like Coca-Cola
➤ Run the operation with half the cost
➤ Have a 'speed boat' organization rather than an 'ocean liner'
➤ Go paperless
➤ Be so good it will be a Harvard case study

The language matters

The language of the word-picture goal really matters. Use language that accesses the right brain and can help fire up some emotion and commitment.

Do not use dry logic to which people can only become intellectually committed at best. This doesn't engage the imagination at all, in fact it deadens it.

When step-change goals are considered for market share, it is interesting how easy it is for the number 2, 3, 4 or 5 brands in the marketplace to picture a goal that creates action and energy. What do they aspire to? 'Become No. 1.' 'Become market leader.' That's powerful.

By contrast, what do most No. 1 brands say is their objective? You'll get answers like 'Stay No. 1', 'Defend the position successfully', 'Maintain it'.

These are not thrilling, nor do they inspire great actions. They lead to do-nothing, low-risk and hope-to-hold-on strategies. They are nowhere near as powerful as the step-change goal for numbers 2, 3, 4 and 5. And the other brands and organizations will have an advantage in adrenalin flow and creativity to hit their target.

For the leading brand, consider the step-change goal: 'Distance yourself from the rest by 10 share points.' 'Distancing yourself' is a terrific step-change goal for a market leader and can inspire and trigger as much action and energy as the followers get by trying to become No. 1.

Martin Luther King didn't say: 'I have a critical path schedule.'

Moreover, as he urged people towards his dream, Martin Luther King also told them what to move away from. He understood that incrementalism was inhibiting because people would become self-satisfied with seeing small changes as 'progress'. And he used a provocative word-picture to give this message:

Avoid the tranquilizing drug of gradualism.

Words can help. Draw word pictures. Some examples (first quoted in *Built to Last*):

➤ President Kennedy didn't announce 'a strengthening of the moon program'. He said in 1961: 'This nation should commit itself to achieving the goal, before this decade is out, of landing a man on the moon and returning him safely to earth.' He died just two years later, but his words lived on.

➤ In the early 1960s Philip Morris had only a 10 percent market share in cigarettes and held a poor sixth position in the marketplace. Nevertheless, it gave itself a word picture to aim for when it set out to 'become the General Motors of the tobacco industry'. And it did.

➤ In 1907 Henry Ford set out to 'democratize the automobile'. He aimed 'to build a motor car for the great multitude – it will be so low in price that no man making a good salary will be unable to own one – and enjoy with his family the blessing of hours of pleasure in God's great open spaces – everybody will be able to afford one, and everyone will have one. The horse will have disappeared from our highways, the automobile will be taken for granted.'

➤ In the 1950s, the company that was later to become Sony gave itself the goal: 'to change the image around the world of Japanese products as poor in quality'. In 1952, it set out to 'make a pocketable radio'.

➤ Apple set out to achieve 'one person, one computer'.

A step-change goal works best when the words catch people's hearts as well as their heads. Hearts are not captured by numbers, unless they are 'magic' numbers: double it, go for a million, become number one. Make the terminology inspirational.

Don't use the same forms and formats for setting discontinuous goals as you do for forecasts and budgets. If you merely substitute a big number for an incremental number in a report, it will not be inspirational. It will not capture your whole heart and mind.

Instead, make the step-change goal different. Inspirational. Challenging. Don't make it just a bigger number. Put a picture in people's minds, a fire in their bellies. Make it so vivid they can smell it.

Hire the world's four best thinkers

This is a very helpful technique to help yourself and the organization identify a step-change goal.

Imagine that four of the world's best creative, practical thinkers are being made available to you for a month. Assume they have had training in your business and industry so they are full of relevant knowledge.

The question is, what goal would you have them work against? What would you want them to tackle together for a month? What do you have as a goal, a dream or a vision that it would be worth their time and talent?

If you don't have this kind of goal, you aren't thinking big enough. Don't be so stuck in incrementalism you have no use for talent. Form such a goal in your mind now. Force yourself and the organization to come up with something that would be worth the world's four best thinkers working on for a month.

Your personal talents deserve more

Your talents, your skills, your life time shouldn't be wasted on merely incremental purposes. Make your purposes meaningful and use this to generate a picture of step-change compared to where you are now.

The purpose of life is a life of purpose.

Continually ask the purpose of the purpose. What is the purpose of solving a problem or addressing an issue? Then ask what is the purpose of that purpose? And so on, until you get to the highest-order thing at which you should be aiming:

```
        P
        U
        R
PURPOSE
        O F
        S
        E
```

For example, consider a personnel planning meeting in which the immediate purpose is to agree staff moves to fill some upcoming vacant positions. You might achieve this initial purpose quite well and feel pleased. And you would expect to have to repeat the process on an 'as needed' basis.

Alternatively, you could start asking yourself what is the purpose of this initial purpose? Probably to keep the organization running smoothly and possibly also to help develop the skills and careers of the people being moved to fill the vacant positions.

Could you aim to use the opportunity to strengthen the organization substantially? Could you use the opportunity of the vacancies to restructure the jobs?

And if a higher purpose is to develop careers, what else are you doing to get supercharged in this area? Waiting for job vacancies is a relatively incremental approach.

Why do you expect to have to repeat the process again in the not too distant future? Why are the vacancies occurring? Are you focusing enough on retaining people and solving any problems that are causing them to leave?

Asking the purpose of the purpose helps move you off just working to relieve symptoms and starts attacking causes.

Ask the purpose of the purpose, then you'll find yourself addressing the biggest issue you could be tackling. You'll find yourself working on big things that make a difference – rather than being tied up in working on some minor issue which won't make much difference in the grand scheme of things.

Once you've identified the big issue to work on, aim to make a substantial difference by going for step-change performance in that area.

Don't dream vaguely and dread precisely: dream precisely and dread vaguely

A common human and organizational habit is to dream vaguely and dread precisely.

We are vague about the possibilities of future achievement; but we are precise about all the barriers, the negatives, the reasons it can't be done. These come quickly and easily to mind.

The secret of breakthrough results is to do the opposite. Focus precisely on the step-change goal and the step-change strategies that might achieve it. Dream as precisely as you can. Suspend into vagueness the worries and concerns about how difficult it may be. Dread as vaguely as you can.

As you dream precisely, make the dream a place to come from rather than a place to arrive at. Make it what, and how, you want to be, rather than what you may end up being. Your precise future is your step-change goal. Then decide the action needed to create that precise future.

For example, imagine you are launching a new product or service in your local area and you want to generate some launch publicity.

One approach is to leave this as a vague 'wish'. It may be your view that big publicity is unlikely to happen in a massive way because local newspapers and radio stations are inundated with requests for publicity. In fact, you tell yourself as you dread precisely that the chances of getting anyone to give priority to your relatively unimportant new service are very low and you'd end up wasting a lot of time and energy on the project with little to show for it. And, further dreading precisely, even if you get them to agree to some minor mention, the effect on the business would be quite small.

Alternatively, dream precisely and dread vaguely. Which radio station and which newspapers would you love to give you publicity? And what exactly would you love for them to say? And how exactly could you leverage that in your sales material etc.? Dream in your mind the exact ideal you'd love. Dread vaguely; ignore the barriers. Then focus on how you might make that dream come true.

Accept risk

There's no such thing as no risk. There are often more risks involved in doing nothing and hoping prosperity will continue than in taking some action that seems risky. The risks of doing nothing are just less obvious.

However, often a person, or an organization, doesn't act but gets overtaken by events. People and organizations fail to change with the times. These arise because of a hope that by doing nothing and ignoring things, they'll go away.

There is often more risk in trying to aim for incrementalism than in going for breakthrough. But people and organizations don't realize this.

We'll cover in a later chapter the strategy of choosing powerful vs limiting mindsets. But for now, decide to choose the organizational mindset of:

> 'Nothing ventured, nothing gained'
> instead of
> 'Better safe than sorry'

Adapt the following three proverbs, which appeal to the emotions, to help generate the acceptance of risk in going for a step-change goal:

➤ You can't discover new oceans unless you have the courage to lose sight of the shore.

➤ The fruit of a tree is out on the limb.

➤ Behold the turtle – it never makes progress until it sticks its neck out.

Distinguish between a miss and a mistake

There's a whole world of difference between these two concepts, but often middle- and low-performing organizations don't recognize it, let alone emphasize it. Instead, everything that doesn't go as planned, everything that doesn't hit what it was aiming at, is a mistake.

Introduce the concept of a miss, allow people to declare their results a miss rather than a mistake, and many more good things will be tried.

After all, when aiming at a dartboard, we often send our first dart left. We learn from that on the second dart, adjust and perhaps go right. The third dart then tends to be closer to the target.

But were the first two darts mistakes? No, they were misses that we learn from and adjust for the next time. Far better to throw the first dart, learn and adjust, than to be so worried about not hitting the target that the dart never leaves your hand.

As you develop different action steps to try to hit a step-change goal, get the organization to view missing the goal as just that – a miss not a mistake. The mistake would be not to try for the step-change goal in the first place.

Dovetail coil-downs and harvests

Breakthrough results will often not come overnight. Sometimes they also need financial investments to achieve them. Sometimes the ideas you come up will require a short-term downward trend in the financial numbers to achieve a significantly step-changed financial result later.

This is a 'coil-down'. It is coiling down in order to be able to leap very high subsequently – and higher than you could have done if you hadn't coiled down.

For example, Unit A has the following actual results and is currently forecast to continue to do a little better each year. It expects, and is designed to achieve, incremental progress in the three years of the forecast. Indeed each unit, Unit B, Unit C etc., is aiming to do a little bit better each year.

However, by investing in Year 1 – for example by sampling a new product nationally – Unit A will achieve a substantially bigger, more profitable business in Years 2 and 3 than it would have done without the big investment. Year 1 is a 'coil-down' for Unit A.

Unit A	Actuals			Forecast	
	Last year	This year	Year 1	Year 2	Year 3
Incrementalism	25	27	28	30	32
Coil-down	25	27	20	40	43

Breakthrough results for the organization as a whole will come from learning to work together to combine the 'coil-down' of Unit A with a year of harvest in another unit, say Unit B. This way the total organization can still achieve the same results as before in Year 1, but is investing on a big breakthrough step for the future.

People will agree to 'harvest', provided that their next year's budget or goal – when they themselves need to 'coil down' – isn't going to be based on improvement on a year when they were on a 'harvest' strategy.

If they don't have this reassurance, they won't harvest for others; they will try to squirrel away reserves for themselves and simultaneously keep the base low. Give them this reassurance and you can 'dovetail'.

In this example, Unit B was planning to improve incrementally each year. But to dovetail with Unit A, it will aim for Year 1 to be a harvest year. And in Year 2, Unit B will itself coil down to get substantially better results from Year 3.

Unit B	Actuals			Forecast	
	Last year	This year	Year 1	Year 2	Year 3
Incrementalism	54	58	62	65	68
Harvest (H)/ coil-down (CD)	54	58	70 H	58 CD	82

Dovetailing these two units' results will lead to breakthrough, compared to the previous system of each and every unit looking for incremental improvement each year.

Total Units A + B	Actuals			Forecast	
	Last year	This year	Year 1	Year 2	Year 3
Incrementalism	79	85	90	97	100
Dovetail	79	85	90	98	125

By Year 3 profits are 25 percent higher than they would have been, and from there will grow at an ever-increasing pace compared to the incremental pathway.

There is a breakthrough difference between these two approaches. In the first, incremental strategy, each part of the organization stays in the status quo, happy to be doing a little bit better, with no thinking big or acting big.

In the second, dovetailing strategy, each unit thinks big and comes up with bold changes that may involve a 'coil-down' year. But by dovetailing with deliberate harvests, the organization can still meet overall the same forecast results as before in the first two years – while putting in place major investments in each of Units A and B which will drive profits up a further 25 percent in Year 3.

Set step-change goals not stretch goals

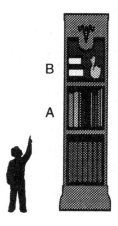

Here is a man by a bookcase. If the book to be reached is set at shelf A, just about out of reach, what will happen? Figuratively speaking, the organization will learn to stretch just a little further, possibly learning to stand on tiptoe. For a stretch goal, an organization will not consider different actions, just try a little bit harder with current actions.

If the book to be reached is set at shelf B, way out of reach, what will happen? Part of the organization may learn to jump. Another part may think of using a chair to stand on. And, who knows, a third part may invent a ladder.

Remember, this is the key difference between aiming for step-change and aiming for incrementalism. It is impossible to reach shelf B by incrementalism. You have to consider alternative actions. It is clear that by simply stretching further, shelf B can never be reached.

This is critical. Many individuals and organizations believe that business progress can still be like a geographical journey between Point A and Point B, say 100 miles away.

On a journey, one can choose to go fast – by car in three hours or even by plane in half an hour. But there is also the possibility of walking 4 miles a day and taking 25 days to get there. Point B will still be reached.

Business and life are not like a geographical journey. The rate of change is so fast that aiming to go at 4 miles a day is not a guarantee that you will ever reach Point B. You can't extrapolate over 25 days. The situation will have changed. Competition will have seen you coming. Someone else will have gone by car, by plane or even beaten you by bike. Discontinuous methods will win. Discontinuous actions will get to places that incrementalism will never reach.

A sporting example: better golf

Let's assume you are a reasonably good golfer, say with a handicap of 20, which means that you score regularly in the low 90s.

You want to get better. What action steps do you think of to get better? Typically, for a business person, they might be as follows:

➤ Play more regularly
➤ Do some practice
➤ Take a lesson from the professional to correct a fault
➤ Perhaps buy some new clubs, which will help at least psychologically.

Taking these action steps, you will get better. Your handicap will go down from 20 to 19 to 18 or so. And you will start scoring in the high 80s rather than the low 90s.

This, however, is a strategy of incrementalism. You are a medium handicap golfer and you are aiming to become a better medium handicap golfer.

That is a very different strategy to dreaming: 'What would I settle for if I knew I couldn't fail? I'd like to break 80 regularly. I'd like a single-figure handicap. I'd love that. I'd settle for that. I'd die happy knowing I'd become a single-figure handicap golfer.'

This second goal of becoming a single-figure handicap golfer, and breaking 80 regularly, is very different. It is step-change. It has two effects. It drives a different sort of fire, energy and enthusiasm. It also changes the logical action steps you would then think of, compared to those you had devised for incremental improvement:

➤ Instead of playing more regularly, you would play less and devote yourself to a period of practice to change your swing totally.
➤ Instead of doing some practice, you would aim to practice intensively.
➤ Instead of spending money on new clubs, you would spend the money on a full course of lessons from a professional teacher.
➤ Instead of going to the teacher with the aim of correcting a small fault in one lesson, you would commit yourself to a series of lessons over several months, during which you would aim to remodel your swing completely.

The point is that choosing a step-change goal generates completely different action steps than choosing to go for being just a little better.

In this case, two medium handicap golfers, of the same standard, in the same golf club, one going for incrementalism, one going for step-change, would end up doing such different things that they might not encounter one another week to week.

But the outcome would be this: the golfer aiming only to be a little better will at best get a little better, because he or she hasn't decided on any action steps that would produce anything different. The golfer aiming for step-change might not get all the step-change he or she wants, but would get substantially better scores than the first golfer because the different action steps were designed to get substantially better scores.

Picturing a step-change, breakthrough achievement will undoubtedly end in better results than if you only aim for a small improvement versus the status quo.

A further sporting example:
the Olympics

I was a good enough hockey player to get into the preliminary squad for Great Britain for the 1972 Munich Olympics. Unfortunately I wasn't good enough to make the final party, but I was with the squad long enough to understand its approach to planning for success.

Britain had not been very successful in previous Olympics. Sixteen teams each year made the Olympics. I cannot remember exactly, but let us assume Britain's previous results had been something like:

1960, Rome – 13th
1964, Tokyo – 15th
1968, Mexico – 14th

What would we aim for in Munich?

An incremental manager might take that data and establish the base period, as follows:

	Rome 1960	Base period Tokyo 1964	Mexico 1968	Average	Goal Munich 1972
Position	13th	15th	14th	14th	?
Index				100	

The average for the base period is 14th. What should be the goal for Munich? One might conclude that a 15 percent improvement, representing a climb of two places over the base period, would be brilliant. After all, such an achievement could be more than celebrated as:

➤ A climb of 2 places, a 15 percent improvement.
➤ More than the average improvement likely in the British teams across all sports.
➤ And an **all-time-record**, better than had ever been done in 60 years!

		Base period			Goal
	Rome 1960	Tokyo 1964	Mexico 1968	Average	Munich 1972
Position	13th	15th	14th	14th	12th
Index				100	115

I'm sure you don't need me to tell you that the squad never approached the Olympics that way.

There's only one reason you would give up several years of your life, there's only one reason you go to the Olympics, there's only one aim for each of the top teams there, and that's:

GET GOLD

If the recommendation on a target had ever been written, it would have deliberately obliterated any thought of being restricted by the base period of the past, and simply focused on the goal as follows:

GOAL
Munich
1972
GOLD!

You know that aiming for 12th, even though it's 15 percent better, wouldn't even get you out of bed, let alone get you out of bed at 5 am, or take you out in the freezing rain to run up sand dunes two and a half years before the event! **Gold** is what will make you do that, nothing less. Gold is what you aim for.

This is not just about motivation and enthusiasm. It's also about

logical action steps. If you are the manager, you would identify different action steps if you are going for gold than if you're going for a 15
percent improvement. For gold, you would add an extra year of
preparatory training. You'd book more pre-Olympic qualifying tour-
naments. And you'd select different players. You'd select good and very
promising players who could attend the whole preparatory program
and who would then end up outstanding.

By taking all these different action steps, the team will end up
higher than it would have done if it had just set out to go for 12th.
This second sporting example is provided because it illustrates well
three lessons:

> The type of the goal you put in your mind determines the sort of
action steps you develop.

> Performance in the past shouldn't be allowed to interfere with set-
ting goals for the future. No individual or team preparing for the
Olympics lets the performance last time dictate the goal this time.
They dissociate themselves from the past and create their own future.

> There's nothing shameful in aiming high and missing. Going for
gold and getting bronze is not failure - it's a different degree of success. In this case, even going for gold and getting sixth is not failure at all — it's success and a bigger success than would be achieved
by other means.

Why it works

Why does setting step-change goals generate significantly different
creativity in devising more stretching action steps that would not have
been thought of otherwise? Consider the paperclip exercise:

THE PAPERCLIP EXERCISE

The purpose of this exercise is to identify as many things as possible for which you could use a paperclip.

Step 1

Give yourself one minute exactly and write down all the things you can think of for which you could use a paperclip. Write them here, now:

Count how many you came up with.

Step 2

Now give yourself another minute and write down all the things you can think of for which you could not use a paperclip. Write down everything that comes to mind, even if subsequently you could think of a way you could use a paperclip for that purpose.

What can we learn from this exercise?

Step 1 is often a largely incremental exercise. You think of things that are an extension of the way you currently use a paperclip, e.g. it can be used as a hairclip; unravel it for a toothpick etc.

Step 2 is different. As you try to think of things you couldn't use a paperclip for, your mind almost automatically does a 'quality check' to see if that is really true. It scans the imagination to see if there could be a connection. For example, you might have thought you couldn't use a paperclip as a hat. But then your mind will realize that you could flatten and thin down a very big paperclip until it was like a sheet of foil and once you have a sheet of foil, of course, you could fold it and make a hat, of sorts.

In Step 2, you set up the impossible and then can challenge your mind to see if there is a way to make it possible. This generates far more ways to use a paperclip than the incremental approach in Step 1, and far more different uses that would never have been devised by your mind under an incremental approach.

The brain can create all sorts of connections – but only when challenged to do so. As an illustration, take any word at random in the dictionary and see if you can find another word to which your brain can't make any connection from the first word. It's impossible.

Setting up the impossible and challenging your mind to find a way to get there from where you are is the secret of why setting step-change goals gets great results.

The Second Thinking Strategy

Build knowhow

versus

Drown in information

4 *Building Knowhow*

Japanese companies have been successful because of their skills and expertise at organizational knowledge creation – the capability of a company as a whole to create new knowledge, disseminate it throughout the organization, and embody it in products, services and systems.

Nonaka and Takeuchi,
The Knowledge Creating Company

Now that you have pictured a step-change, the second part of tri△ngular thinking is to search for the knowledge that will help you achieve it – to build knowhow.

The concept of **knowhow** goes beyond knowledge. It is **applicable knowledge**, knowledge that will help you achieve the step-change goal you've set. This is in contrast to accumulating knowledge for its own sake or as an end in itself.

The strategy of building knowhow comes ahead of the strategy of creative thinking because it helps all your subsequent creative thinking to be based on reality. It helps you keep things practical and ensure that the resultant action steps will end in great breakthrough results.

Moreover, there are often many ideas already available that you could simply adapt, if you only knew about them. You may not need to reinvent the wheel.

Recall also that this is the way the brain naturally works. When faced with the challenge of leaving the high-jump and considering how to get over a far higher bar, the brain first scanned for knowledge of other systems that could achieve that height. And it quickly came up with ideas like the pole-vault, trampoline and ladder – before it went on to invent more exotic ways.

The advantage of knowhow

When other organizations beat you in the marketplace or in competition for something, it is often because of their applicable knowledge. 'Knowledge that helps' is often what makes the difference and we recognize this – while somehow offering internally it as an excuse for our comparative failure. We almost view it as cheating. In other words, it's nothing to do with our skill or abilities – the other side just happened to know things we didn't.

Consider a situation where you may be competing for permission to develop a building on a particular site. On the one hand, your proposal has been impeccably prepared, wonderfully argued and submitted in a way that is completely consistent with the established procedure. On the face of it, you feel, your proposal is better than the competitors' and should be accepted. However, you lose out, not because your proposal didn't have merit, but because a competitor 'knew the right people'. They knew who were going to be the key decision makers, what their biases were, and they were able to influence them more effectively as a result.

And this made the difference. We use phrases like:

➤ They must have inside knowledge
➤ They knew all the tricks of the trade
➤ They certainly knew what they were doing
➤ They had the advantage of local knowledge

➤ They must have known something in advance
➤ They knew something no one else did
➤ They really knew their way around
➤ They knew the right person.

This is the sort of knowhow that will help you achieve step-change results.

Knowledge vs information

Knowledge is different to information. Knowledge is a far bigger asset in achieving step-change results. However, more and more individuals and organizations are getting bogged down in sifting and sorting masses and masses of information. The more energy and time are spent doing this, the less are spent on building really good knowhow. The organization needs to learn to bypass information to get to knowhow.

To get breakthrough results, therefore, you need to bring both parts of the second thinking strategy alive: you need to become both passionate about building knowhow and angry at drowning in information pollution.

Let us draw the contrast between information and knowledge and then identify ways to build the applicable knowledge which will help achieve breakthrough results.

Information

Historically, communication was relatively sparse and slow and a business could gain a competitive edge by having more information.

This is no longer true. Information is both abundant and accessible.

It is easy for everyone to produce incredible quantities of facts and figures, organized and analyzed every which way.

In fact, we already have too much information. Many organizations
look like this:

INFORMATION INFORMATION INFORMATION INFORMATION
INFORMATION INFORMATION INFORMATION INFORMATION
INFORMATION INFORMATION INFORMATION INFORMATION
INFORMATION INFORMATION INFORMATION INFORMATION
INFORMATION INFORMATION INFORMATION INFORMATION
INFORMATION INFORMATION INFORMATION INFORMATION
INFORMATION INFORMATION INFORMATION INFORMATION
INFORMATION INFORMATION INFORMATION INFORMATION
INFORMATION INFORMATION INFORMATION INFORMATION
INFORMATION INFORMATION INFORMATION INFORMATION
INFORMATION INFORMATION INFORMATION INFORMATION
INFORMATION INFORMATION INFORMATION INFORMATION

Having more information will not give you a sustainable competitive
edge. In fact, more and more information will actually hurt rather than
help. It is like salt on your food. None is too little; there is an amount
that makes things just right; adding more makes the food inedible.
Perhaps it is like this for you already. How much of your time do you
already find yourself in the righthand column?

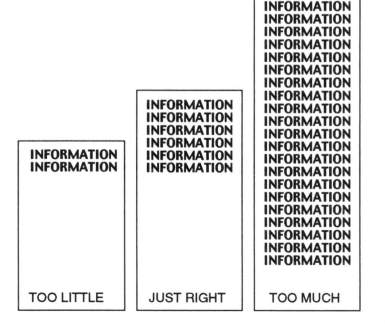

TOO LITTLE   JUST RIGHT   TOO MUCH

Information pollution

A good mental exercise is to establish the least helpful information you are provided with each day and get furious about it.

Here is one candidate. When you fly long distance they show you a screen with a map of the flight and information such as current speed, headwind, altitude, expected time at destination. Much of this is useful: particularly time of arrival, how long to go in the flight and local time. But who on earth needs to know that the outside temperature at 35,000 feet is −37°C? Who is going to think based on that, 'Oh dear, I haven't brought my winter woollies, so I can't go for a walk on the wing'?

Why are we given the information that the outside temperature is −37°C? Because it is available. Because it is being monitored for technical reasons and because it is technically possible to pass on all the information that is being monitored. But the passing on of this useless-to-us information delays the provision of selected information that is helpful, such as latest expected time of arrival. And we all sit there, tolerating the information pollution without complaint.

This syndrome is happening in your organization today and spreading like a virus at an unstoppable rate. We need to resist, deter and turn back information pollution.

THE JUNK MAIL TEST

Ask a group in your organization: 'Hands up, how many of you receive junk mail?' Everyone will put their hand up.

Now ask the same group: 'Hands up, how many of you send junk mail?' No one will put their hand up.

So you have an organization where everyone receives junk mail and nobody sends it. Interesting.

What's the difference between knowledge and information?

Knowledge is significantly better than information. And that is good news for you, because you probably already operate with knowledge rather than just information.

The three-part acid test

There is a three-part acid test which can help you decide whether you're dealing with knowledge or just information. It was first devised by Theodore Rosak in *The Cult Information*.

Knowledge is:

➤ created in **individual** minds
➤ drawing on individual **experience**
➤ separating the **significant** from the **irrelevant**.

If the material passes this three-part acid test, the chances are you are dealing with knowledge. If not, you're probably just processing information.

Examples of the difference between knowledge and information

Newspaper headline

The headline reads: 'New supermarket chain to create 800 jobs.' The article announces plans for a major supermarket chain to build new megastores in the area and employ 800 people. This is information. The information implies that this event is good for employment by creating jobs. If your brain is in neutral, operating only on the basis of information, you will accept this implication and move on to the next page.

However, insist that your brain operates in knowledge mode: what happens?

Remember, knowledge is created in individual minds, drawing on individual experience, separating the significant from the irrelevant. What does your experience tell you? Your experience recognizes that people in this situation are unlikely to make more purchases than before, they'll just make them in a supermarket instead of smaller stores.

Knowledge recognizes that, inherently, the purpose of the supermarket is to be more efficient at handling purchases than the stores in which these things were previously bought.

Knowledge therefore suggests a decline in the total jobs available – whereas the information, at face value, would imply the opposite.

What is an acre?

An acre is a measurement of land area. How big is it?

Answer A: An acre is 4047 square meters or 4840 square yards.

That is good, correct information. But you are none the wiser for knowing that information.

Answer B: An acre is about the size of a football field.

That is knowledge. And it is more useful.

Indeed, for the rest of your life, if you ever encounter the term 'acre' you will remember it, usefully, as being the size of a football field. By contrast, you have probably already forgotten how many square yards it is.

Case law

The legal profession also helps illustrate the vast difference between information and knowledge. The information available on case law is almost limitless. Every meaningful case in every jurisdiction is written up, forming huge law libraries. The information is abundant and accessible to all lawyers.

But knowledge of the law is different. Knowledge involves separating the significant from the irrelevant. Therefore knowledge involves being able to focus on those cases and situations most helpful and relevant to the one you're working on. This is a very real and valuable asset. This asset is tacit knowledge, in the minds of particular lawyers. It is why you might go to one lawyer for a case on one subject, but choose a completely different lawyer for another case – even though the same information is available to both.

An example: knowledge of consumers vs information about consumers

Many questionnaires designed to get feedback from consumers are only ever likely to get information and will miss out on the all-important knowledge. This is partly because they are designed for people to give a rational, logical explanation of their views and decisions, when in reality these are based as much on emotion, feeling and hunch.

Secondly, questionnaires are designed to transmit the basis of these views and decisions via logical phrases, when in reality the consumer uses visual cues, triggers and feelings, often almost without thinking, certainly without rationalization.

A parallel may be the way you know your spouse or close family. You know them 'like the back of your hand'. You know exactly what they are thinking and how they will respond.

Getting more and more information about consumer decisions and views is unlikely to produce step-change results. Getting more helpful knowledge will.

So, if you are selling mouthwash, it is helpful to know that people really want to avoid, at all costs, the stigma of bad breath – even though they'll tell you they want nice-smelling breath. There's a huge difference between the two.

If you are selling perfumes, it is helpful to know not only that some are used by women as 'man-catchers' but also that women can recognize the subtle body signals coming from a man when he's attracted by the perfume. And that's how they'll judge it, even though they may tell you, in the logical question-and-answer questionnaire, that they like the smell of that fragrance personally or that it stays on.

If you are selling haircare products for men, it is helpful to know that many men don't want their hair noticed, one way or the other: they don't want it to look either as if it needs a wash or so good that it distracts attention from other things they consider more important. But they may tell you in the questionnaire that they like their hair a certain way, because they think this is how they ought to feel about their hair.

A further example: knowledge of how things work vs information about how things work

In most organizations there is a huge difference between the information about how the organization works and the knowledge of how it really works in practice.

The information given out about how an organization works is probably full of official procedures, rules and processes to follow. Roles and responsibilities are outlined. Organization charts are prepared. But how things get done is often very different in practice. People have found that the rules don't always work. They need to be adjusted for different personalities and different interactions between people. What works for one person won't work for the next. What works between two people won't work with another two, and so on. Often, on many things, the secretary has the power and influence, not the boss!

Knowledge of 'how things work around here' will help an individual get far better results than any amount of information about how they are *meant* to work. Knowledge like this is not just effective in your own organization, it also influences third parties – whether it be an organization you sell to, buy from, cooperate with, need the support of, need to influence, need approval from or whatever.

Is more and more information innocent and harmless?

There seems to be no such thing as innocent information. This is illustrated by the previous example of the newspaper headline: 'New supermarket chain to create 800 jobs'. The headline was written with 'top-spin', originating in the public relations department, to put the best possible light on the event.

With so much information available, much of it has to be summarized or put into headline form for us to absorb it. The trouble is that the headline or summary is often made with an end in mind and so obscures the real knowledge.

Never ask the barber if you need your hair cut.

Every day you get information:

➤ you didn't ask for
➤ that isn't in your best interest
➤ presented in such a psychologically persuasive manner that it's used in your decision making without you realizing it.

We each receive more information in one day than a seventeenth-century person received in an entire lifetime.

In any organization there is not only more and more data available from the traditional sources, but information is also coming from more and more new sources.

Thus the business day can be full of reports and e-mails, each richer and richer with facts and figures, manipulated and compiled every which way. There may be hard copies as well as electronic copies. And each of these can be copied to multiple people and multiple parts of the organization.

The three eras of information

We have rapidly moved from the era of helpful information to the era of overload and we are now in the era of pollution.

HELPFUL INFORMATION

INFORMATION OVERLOAD

INFORMATION POLLUTION

One of the reasons this has happened is to do with the relative balance of time taken to compose and deliver a message versus the time taken to read it.

The time taken to compose and deliver a message used to far exceed the time taken to absorb it. In Roman times, delivering a message took months. The number of messages sent was relatively few. But these were each helpful, often eagerly awaited.

More recently, a letter to a loved one – away at war, or in a distant place – was eagerly awaited. It took time to compose it well, with much thought and many rewrites and false starts, and time to deliver it.

Even very recently, in a normal office, it took longer to compose a letter and send it, copied to a few recipients, than it took for each recipient to read it. Offices were concerned with raising the efficiency of their output.

THE ERA OF HELPFUL INFORMATION

TIME TAKEN

| COMPOSE | SEND | | READ |

All suddenly changed and we moved to the era of information overload.

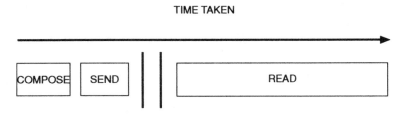

THE ERA OF INFORMATION OVERLOAD

Personal computers and e-mail have changed things considerably. It is possible now to type in a quick message, attach to it back-up files of related messages and, at the push of a button, transmit the whole file to a plethora of other people. And all this can be done far faster than the recipients can absorb it.

But the overload era has rapidly led to information pollution. Just because it is so easy and fast to compose and send information, more and more people do it, more often, to more and more people.

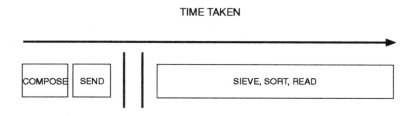

THE ERA OF INFORMATION POLLUTION

We have moved from overload to pollution in the twinkling of an e-mail. Now we need filters to sift and sort the incoming information. In just a few short years, we have moved from needing a secretary to help output, to needing no secretary, to needing a secretarial device to sort the input.

So material is transmitted rapidly around the world, around our organizations and from person to person. Will we allow it to be just information or information with top-spin? Or will we insist on using technology to focus on building knowhow?

For breakthrough results, the answer is clear. Insist on building knowhow. Do not allow people to assume that more and more information is a good thing, nor that it is acceptable because it is well intentioned. The key is to assume that polluting others with information is a sin. It is swamping them and they don't have time and energy to focus on what they should be doing. The key to achieving breakthrough results is to get furious with information pollution and eradicate it before it starts.

At the same time, focus single-mindedly on building knowhow, the specific knowledge that will help you achieve those breakthrough results.

Building knowhow

Once you know what your step-change breakthrough objectives are, it is quite remarkable how very easy and effective it is to focus on building the base of useful knowledge to help you achieve them if you aren't drowning in information.

What is the knowhow that is most relevant to your goals? Let's take some simple examples:

➤ If your purpose is to beat a particular competitor, many individuals and organizations start off by trying to gain information on that competitor. However, that's not knowhow. The knowhow you need is how to *beat* the competitor. So find someone who has beaten them. Find out what they did and try to copy it. If no one has beaten that particular competitor, find a business that won against a similar competitor to yours and aim to emulate what they did.

Simply gaining information on your competitor is like studying all the muscles and armor of Goliath. All that will do is make your organization paralyzed as it learns how strong Goliath is. Instead, study how David beat Goliath and use that knowhow.

➤ If you decide on a step-change objective of dramatically increasing your 'consumption' in a market – as opposed to incrementally increasing your share of current purchases – then study others that have done the same. Gain the knowhow of how Coca-Cola tries to increase its share of drink occasions – including water! Or study how bottled water itself in many countries has created a business from nothing – just by increasing its share of drinking occasions.

Set a step-change objective to drive your throat drop business to 20 percent of all 'fidget' occasions and the most applicable knowledge may well not come from studying other throat drop brands – but from studying Coca-Cola.

You can see how the combination of picturing a step-change objective and then seeking applicable knowledge will lead to completely different action steps. If you had just aimed to sell a few more throat drops than last year, you wouldn't even consider the knowhow you could learn from Coca-Cola or bottled water.

➤ If your step-change, breakthrough objective is to produce and market products that can sell at twice the price, then seek out other products that are sold at twice the price and emulate them.

For example, if you are marketing cosmetics and toiletries, don't focus for pricing information on your current competitors in the mass market. Instead, focus on gaining applicable knowhow from the prestige or luxury market. Examine the principles and practices that succeed – packaging, service, image, personal attention – and then consider how you could emulate some of them.

If all you were after was a way to sell your products at a 5 or 10 percent higher price, you would be trapped into a very narrow range of learning. And, indeed, you might decide not to increase the price by 5 or 10 percent, because of previous bad experiences at increasing prices. It is the very discontinuous nature of the goal that causes you to seek knowhow of who has done it and suggests the opportunity to adopt the action steps they did. And so you've identified a possible way to achieve your goal.

Tacit and explicit knowledge

One systemic way to build knowhow is based on the work of Nonaka and Takeuchi in *The Knowledge Creating Company*. There is a big opportunity, however, to turn such a theory into practical action – to turn it into things that are Monday morning do-able.

Breakthrough results will come from building two forms of knowledge – **tacit** knowledge and **explicit** knowledge.

Tacit knowledge

Tacit knowledge is the build-up of an individual's experiences. An organization is the sum of the individuals within it. Most of the knowledge an organization possesses is the sum of the tacit knowledge in individual heads. Tacit knowledge comes from experience. It includes insights and understandings. It is what generates gut feelings, intuition and hunches. It comes from being in touch with a particular fashion or target group. It is the wealth of expertise that comes from 20 years of relevant experience. It drives personal beliefs and perspectives.

Explicit knowledge

Explicit knowledge is the overt expression of knowledge. It is the formal articulated systems that explain how things work. Explicit knowledge is found in formulae, written-down methods, instruction manuals, written best practices, instructional videotapes, lectures or presentations on how to do things.

Building knowhow

Knowhow comes from building up, and transferring within the organization, both the tacit and the explicit knowledge that will help achieve the goal. So, for example, an insight that is highly personal is of far higher value to the organization – and will produce more discontinuous results – if the individual converts it into explicit knowledge and so allows it to be shared with others.

Alternatively, one individual may have great tacit knowledge of a subject. Another individual may have a comparable amount of tacit knowledge that is in many respects different. If the two tacit knowledge holders engage on the subject they are likely to produce even more valuable insights, or knowhow, than would be produced if they kept their tacit knowledge in separate silos.

Consider the issue of building consumption of a product in developing markets and the role that package size plays. Different managers may have different experiences of this. One manager may have experienced success with very small, single-use sizes like sachets.

Here the low unit cost makes the product affordable for those for whom low cash outlay is key. And through making sachets available, both availability of the product and consumption build.

Another manager in another country may have opposite experience and knowledge on the subject: in that country consumers go for bulk sizes because they perceive them to be more economical, and perhaps also believe that prices will rise in the future because of inflation. So they buy in bulk and that builds consumption.

When both managers engage on the issue of how best to build consumption through sizing, they'll each end up with better knowledge of ways to do this, of when each method works best.

As a different example of knowledge transfer, an individual with no knowledge can rapidly build applicable knowledge by seeking out all the explicit knowledge available. This means searching in a focused way for what's available both within the organization and often, productively, outside of it in other areas such as professional bodies.

The individual without knowledge can also search for the tacit knowledge holders – and request and insist that they make their tacit knowledge explicit. This is the equivalent of 'give me your 20 years' experience in 20 days'.

The four systemic ways of building knowhow

There are four systemic ways to develop the specific knowhow that will help achieve your goals. Pursue these specifically and aggressively.

Tacit to tacit

This form of building involves sharing experiences and wisdom between people who know something about an area. This happens, for example, informally between sessions at a conference. But there is a huge opportunity to seek out other tacit knowledge holders proactively and regularly and engage with them.

Tacit to explicit

This form involves converting tacit experience to explicit knowledge so that it can be used by other people. This happens, for example, when franchise operations write down success models for others to follow. Once again, there is a real opportunity to identify tacit knowledge that will really help towards a goal and get it made explicit.

Explicit to tacit

This involves helping individuals internalize knowledge from explicit knowledge models. For example, flight simulators are very effective in training pilots; people can find out about mindmapping from the Internet. Proactive, vigorous searching for relevant explicit knowledge will pay huge dividends.

Explicit to explicit

This includes combining different kinds of explicit knowledge from several different areas to create new knowledge. For example, technologies from different businesses can be combined to create a new product approach.

This four-way model provides an excellent framework for any individual to identify what they could do to help build the knowhow that will help achieve a discontinuous goal. It provides a roadmap. The better job that is done in each of these four areas, the better the chances of building the knowhow that will help achieve breakthrough results.

You don't know what you don't know

One of the biggest barriers to building knowhow, however, is that people think they know how others have achieved things, but in fact they don't. They think they know all there is to know, but they don't. As a result, they don't take specific action to know more, to build applicable knowhow.

Even worse, this in-built arrogance can lead to failure to apply something that might work. It's relatively easy to assume, mistakenly, that you understand someone else's tacit knowledge, in a way that rejects it as relevant to your issue.

MIND-OPENING PRACTICE:
DO YOU KNOW WHAT YOU DON'T KNOW?

There follows a trivia quiz of 10 questions (adapted from Dawson's *Decision Making*). You don't need to know the exact answers. For each question, you just need to give a high and a low estimate, such that you are 90 percent sure the answer will be within the range you have quoted. You can go as low or as high as you wish. Your aim is to only get one answer outside these ranges.

90 percent confidence range

		Low	High
1	Martin Luther King's age at his death	30 39	50 ✓
2	Length of the Nile River	1 mile	150 miles ✓187
3	Number of countries that are members of OPEC	4 13	50 ✓
4	Number of books in the Old Testament	10 39	50 ✓
5	Diameter of the moon in miles	400	1500 2160
6	Weight of an empty Boeing 747 in lbs	100,000 390,000	1,000,000 ✓
7	Year in which Wolfgang Amadeus Mozart was born	1500 1756	1800 ✓
8	Air distance from London to Tokyo	1000	5000 5850
9	Gestation period (in days) of an Asian elephant	200	600 645
10	Deepest (known) point in the oceans (in feet)	39,000 36	45000 ✓

Yes, you don't know the exact answers, but do try to give a range. Don't move on until you've done so. Remember, the purpose of this mind opener is to give ranges you think are 90 percent right and you can go as low and as high as you wish. You need to get no more than one answer outside these ranges.

See the next page for the answers before reading further.

520
7
37400

ANSWERS – DO YOU KNOW WHAT YOU DON'T KNOW?

1	39 years
2	4187 miles
3	13 countries
4	39 books
5	2160 miles
6	390,000 lbs
7	1756
8	5959 miles
9	645 days
10	36,198 feet

For how many questions did you provide a big enough range to accommodate the answer? Was it nine or fewer?

Why on earth would you have fewer than nine answers within the range? After all, you could quote as low or as high as you wished. In such circumstances, why would you end up wrong?

The answer lies in your arrogance and overconfidence. Even though you know you don't know, you think you can work it out. You probably used some way of guessing or estimating the right answer based on rough perception or feeling. You then have trouble in imagining that your first impression could be very far out.

Admit to yourself as an operating principle that you don't know what you don't know. Open your mind to the fact and seek to build applicable knowhow.

Building knowhow: Interhead as well as Internet

In the future, the organizations that achieve breakthrough results will be those that make effective use of the 'Interhead' as well as the Internet. The Interhead is a made-up term for the web of connections between people in the organization, the 'meeting of minds', the ability to interact to produce better results. The better the Interhead an organization builds, the better the knowhow it will build towards achieving step-change results.

The Interhead needs to function well in building knowhow. First, it needs to find ways to make tacit knowledge explicit. That's the equivalent of a cranial computer taking material from memory, organizing it in a user-friendly way and displaying it on the screen with exciting graphics and easy-to-follow instructions. The material is no use if it remains in the desktop memory – in the same way, it's no use if it's left in the memory of a single cranial computer. And it's only of real use if it is accessible and relevant, otherwise it won't be applied by others. Moreover, there needs to be a 'help' system for when users are stuck.

The Interhead also needs to build knowhow by allowing the tacit knowledge in the memory of one cranial computer to be added to the tacit knowledge in the memory of another, and then sorting the total in a way that generates more and better knowhow than the two isolated silos. This is in much the same way as computers work together to form the Internet.

Similarly, the Interhead must be an active system where people proactively search for the explicit knowledge available in the organization to help them achieve their step-change goals. They need to have a menu of what explicit knowledge is available, arranged by helpful themes – a form of internal *Yellow Pages*. And there must be means of browsing and searching that knowledge.

Finally, the Interhead needs to find ways of comparing the explicit knowledge that comes from one cranial computer with the output from others in different areas to build knowhow through comparison.

Of course, there will be many barriers to building an effective Interhead and making effective connections between cranial computers to produce applicable knowhow. For example, there's a cranial computer virus called NIH, not-invented-here syndrome. There are also often programs in the receiving cranial computer called restricted mindsets that search for ways it can't be done, that find out from history that 'we've tried it before and it won't work'. Some cranial computers are programmed to reject input from other specific cranials – either individuals they have no respect for or organizational functions that have lost credibility, for example 'Headquarters is out of touch, so much of their advice is unhelpful.'

Other blockages to an effective Interhead are caused by some people not wanting to share their knowledge because keeping it to themselves gives them a personal competitive edge. And there are repeated blockages caused by the software of one cranial computer not interacting well with another cranial because they're on different 'wavelengths'.

So to achieve breakthrough results you need to take action to construct an effective Interhead to build specific knowhow that will contribute towards your goals through the generation of both tacit and explicit knowledge.

10 principles to help build knowhow

Here are 10 principles to follow in your day-to-day work that will help build the knowhow you need to hit a step-change objective. The more of these you and your organization use, the more often you'll build helpful knowhow.

---

1   Engage with peers rather than staying in polite silos
2   Discuss the contradictions
3   Seek knowledge holders as well as position holders
4   Treat the boss as a tacit knowledge holder
5   Celebrate knowledge transfer rather than pretend from first principles
6   Seek and interview others with tacit knowledge
7   Proactively seek out all explicit sources
8   Make your tacit knowledge explicit
9   Ridicule the barriers to knowledge transfer
10 Keep your goals in the forefront of your mind

Engage with peers rather than staying in polite silos

You need those with good tacit knowledge of a subject to engage with each other to produce better knowhow. This helps separate out superstition from knowledge. It builds new understanding rapidly.

This is particularly helpful at senior levels of an organization. That is where a lot of tacit knowledge resides and it is from here that much of the direction of the organization comes.

At the same time, it is often at the senior level that there is a habit and practice of polite non-engagement. If it is not specifically your responsibility, there may be a tendency not to comment or engage with peers. But this leads you to miss out on utilizing the organization's assets of tacit knowledge.

Sometimes there is also a historical tendency to think that knowledge is power. So you keep your knowledge to yourself, in case the knowledge you have, that others don't, can come in useful later or can be used as security for your own position.

Finding a way to overcome the above tendencies will help produce breakthrough results. Move to a habit and practice of engagement between those with tacit knowledge to produce significantly better, new knowhow.

Discuss the contradictions

Most knowhow is to be found in the contradiction of rules or truisms. Anyone can follow a rule or slogan, right out the window. Great results will come from knowing when not to, indeed when to do the opposite.

The best knowhow lies in the contradictions between apparent rules, the contradictions between different advice offered, the contradictions with your own experience.

But take any group of people, any team, any organization, and they are likely to talk about anything and everything but the contradictions they faced and the contradictions they generate. Perhaps people shy away from it because it might appear confrontational.

Yet this is where the great learning is – understanding when to do one, when to do the other; understanding the experience of others and why they might follow a different rule.

Take as an example the US Marines. They have made great strides in passing on tacit knowledge to operate by, as opposed to relying on instructions and commands from HQ. Their best three pieces of tacit knowledge are:

➤ Keep on the move
➤ Use surprise
➤ Take the high ground.

This is excellent tacit knowledge and can be used effectively in any engagement anywhere in the world. But a higher level of knowledge lies in the contradictions:

➤ If I take the high ground, but keep on the move, won't I end up on the low ground?
➤ If I keep on the move as the enemy approaches my ambush, won't I lose the element of surprise?

Wherever there are contradictions, there is the potential for a competitive edge through knowhow. Discuss the contradictions.

Seek knowledge holders as well as position holders

Within any organization there is frequently a difference between position holders and the holders of the best tacit knowledge. For example, a newly appointed manager will often have less tacit knowledge of a business than their predecessor who has now moved on to a different position. Moreover, even when someone has spent time on the job, it's a mistake to assume that they are the repository of all the organization's tacit knowledge on that business.

There is often more tacit knowledge in people now working on other businesses or elsewhere in the organization on the same type of business. You need to seek out and engage with all sources of tacit knowledge rather than restrict interaction to the tacit knowledge of a current position holder.

Treat the boss as a tacit knowledge holder

Separate out the roles of your boss and bosses between those of executive decision makers and those of tacit knowledge holders:

- ➤ Ask to have their 20 years' experience in 20 minutes.
- ➤ Ask them not to act as executive at this stage (asking for progress on the project, giving direction) but simply to focus on giving you their knowledge.
- ➤ Then take the knowledge, combine it with what you know and build new knowhow to help you achieve the goal.

Celebrate knowledge transfer rather than pretend from first principles

You probably do not readily acknowledge when your plans and ideas have been influenced by knowledge transfer from others. Rather, you may often pretend to yourself and others that those plans and ideas were reached through a return to basics or a relearning of an old truism. That is not to say that the action, in hindsight, could not have been derived from first principles. But the real process is often different. This pretence is unhelpful and counter-productive on several fronts.

It misses out on the opportunity to reinforce the successful habit of knowledge transfer. It also reinforces the mindset that the best way to move ahead is to work it out cleverly by yourself in your silo. In addition it damages the morale of those involved in providing the knowledge – the glory is stolen without recognition of their contribution.

Seek and interview others with tacit knowledge

Don't just identify them. Don't merely talk to them and hope know-ledge will rub off. Specifically, ask them what they have learnt, what they know, what guidance would they give. Go to 'the horse's mouth' and ask for their knowhow. What one person can do any person has the potential to do.

Proactively seek out all explicit sources

These sources can be reading material, courses, seminars, articles, books, CD-roms, write-ups and, increasingly, the Internet. The key is to seek out explicit sources in areas that will help – rather than waiting for stuff to cross your desk and then select what is useful. Be an active, specific searcher.

Make your tacit knowledge explicit

It is remarkable how effective this is. First, make a commitment to give a talk or a speech or to write an article. This, in turn, produces thought and preparation. Moreover, working out how to explain things to oth-ers forces you first to sort things out in your own mind.

By making your knowledge explicit to others they take it on board and use it to help you. They can't use your knowledge if it's in your head.

Ridicule the barriers to knowledge transfer

NIH, not invented here, is the best known barrier to knowledge trans-fer. Identify it as a disease. Become intensely dissatisfied with individ-uals and organizations that exhibit it. Identify examples of it, publicise them and ridicule them. Make anyone who exhibits NIH a Luddite in today's world.

Keep your goals in the forefront of your mind

Insist that you and your organization return repeatedly to the end result of what you are after. Focus specifically on the knowledge that is applicable. Don't put energy behind building knowledge for its own sake. The purpose is not to become a university of general knowledge. Focus on the knowledge that will get step-change results.

By contrast, it is amazing how often you come across knowledge that will help when you have your goals in mind. The brain receives so many inputs of information and observation that most are necessarily screened out. How often do you find yourself hearing something but not really listening to it? How often do you find yourself in a position where you must have seen something but didn't really notice it? All this is because you've tuned out.

By contrast, how often, once you've decided to do something, do you notice all sorts of opportunities and linkages that will help? Once the family has decided to get a puppy, it's amazing how many 'puppies for sale' signs you notice as you drive past that you otherwise would have seen but not noticed. Moreover, once you have the goal, you both notice the sign and stop the car to investigate.

Remember, build knowhow, don't drown in information.

The Third
Thinking Strategy

Use creative
thinking

versus

Logic alone

5 *Using Creative Thinking*

Creativity, I fear, is a void in many of our organizations. Widespread dissatisfaction among executives over the degree of innovation and creativity in their companies is more common these days than the grey flannel suit.

Robert Galvin, Motorola

Using creative thinking rather than logic alone is the third essential strategy in tri△ngular thinking. It is an essential partner to picturing a step-change and building knowhow if you want to achieve breakthrough results. Just like removing one of the three key essentials of fire (fuel, oxygen and water) will put the fire out, so trying to get breakthrough results without creative thinking simply will not work.

For example, just applying logic to the knowhow you've built won't give you your best chance of breakthrough results. Indeed, using logic alone may be counter-productive. Logic alone can quickly be used to explain why step-change achievement is difficult, to justify why incremental results are reasonable and all that can be expected.

Moreover, putting new knowhow into old, limiting mindsets will result in status quo - it won't generate breakthrough results. There is no point in building knowhow if you are just going to use it to support the box of incrementalism.

GHOSTS DO NOT BLEED

A man was convinced he was a ghost. He was absolutely sure of it. Nothing could convince him otherwise.

His doctor was keen to help change him. She told him to go away for a week and continuously repeat to himself the phrase: 'Ghosts do not bleed.'

The man did so: 'Ghosts do not bleed, ghosts do not bleed', for a week.

A week later, he returned to the doctor repeating: 'Ghosts do not bleed.' At this, the doctor brought out a scalpel and slashed the man's arm. Blood flowed out freely all over his arm.

'There!' said the doctor triumphantly, smiling.

'There!' said the man. 'Ghosts do bleed!'

How much does this happen in your organization?

To get breakthrough results, you need to consider your new knowhow with a fresh, open mind. You need to think creatively and imaginatively on how to use it to achieve step-change. It is the fusion between knowledge and creative thinking, towards a step-change goal, which produces step-change results.

Creative versus logical thinking

Imagination is more important than knowledge. For while knowledge defines all we currently know and understand, imagination points to all we might yet discover and create.

Einstein

Creative thinking involves the addition of **imagination**. That's the key critical difference. If you want to move from logic-only thinking to add creativity, you simply need to access your imagination. Imagination is what makes the difference.

> Our memory tells how the world was,
> Our senses tell us how the world is,
> Our imagination tells us how the world might be.

The secret is to be able to combine imagination with knowledge. Often we are forced to choose between one or the other – either continue with someone who knows the business backwards but is stuck in their ways, or appoint someone who doesn't know the business but will bring a fresh outlook and new ideas.

There are two strategies for using imagination:

➤ break the barriers and boundaries that keep you in the left half of the brain where logic resides
➤ access the right half of the brain where imagination resides.

(See Chapter 7 on becoming whole-brained vs half-brained.)

There is a real, noticeable difference between logic-only, left-brained-only thinking and creative thinking that uses imagination and the right side of the brain. Such a difference has been remarked on down the centuries.

➤ Our thinking creates problems that the same type of thinking will not solve (Einstein)

➤ It is by intuition that we create, it is by logic that we prove (Poincaré)

➤ The logical mind can spot wrong answers, but it takes the creative mind to spot wrong questions

➤ Reason can answer questions, but imagination has to ask them (Ralph N Gerard)

➤ Logic plays within boundaries, imagination plays with boundaries

➤ Discovery consists of looking at the same thing as everyone else and thinking something different

➤ The ultimate solutions to problems are rational, the process of finding them is not

When individuals or organizations have successfully used creative thinking to achieve a result, it often brings a breakthrough that others can only admire (see the expressions overleaf). The problem is that although each solution is admired and logical in hindsight, it needed an imaginative leap to get the solution in the first place. Breakthrough results will come from generating the sort of ideas that not only work, but break through. How can we do this?

There seem to be very few techniques available for creative thinking. Brainstorming comes to mind; attending creativity courses; reading books by De Bono. And that's about the limit for most people. They will perhaps have heard of other books like *A Kick in the Seat of Your Pants* by Roger Oesch. But these seem to be on the wild side of what most people perceive would be helpful to them.

In contrast, there are lots and lots of things to do to promote logical-only thinking. You can occupy yourself by collecting more data; analyzing the numbers; breaking down the numbers; comparing with history. And you can write up the results of your thinking and have a coherent summary or report to show for your thinking efforts. From that can come logical 'indicated actions' to help the business.

Different companies adopt different ways to generate creative

USING CREATIVE THINKING IN ADDITION TO LOGIC

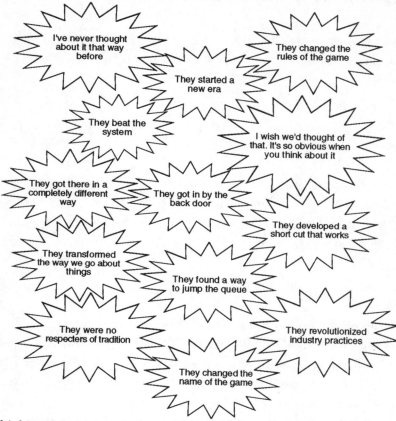

I've never thought about it that way before

They changed the rules of the game

They started a new era

They beat the system

I wish we'd thought of that. It's so obvious when you think about it

They got there in a completely different way

They got in by the back door

They developed a short cut that works

They transformed the way we go about things

They found a way to jump the queue

They were no respecters of tradition

They revolutionized industry practices

They changed the name of the game

thinking, but so far it has been largely trial and error – mostly error.

Some companies, like advertising agencies, split out the creative function from the logical function and form two separate groups of people. The first are called 'creatives' and the second 'account people'. But this is a horrendously expensive approach and moreover fails to achieve that essential combination of creative and logical thinking. You too often end up with work that is creative but won't sell, or is logical but isn't creative.

In contrast, Dana Corporation, an auto parts supply company, does the opposite. There is no separate group, but it involves everybody in the company in a gigantic employee idea-generation program.

The point is that many companies are after creative thinking as well as logical thinking but few have realized how to do it. Tri∆ngular thinking is one solution that can be applied broadly and effectively.

Generating ideas that work: two traps

There are two main traps into which people fall when trying to generate ideas that work and these are extremes at opposite ends of a spectrum.

Trap 1: Trying to work it out logically

The first extreme arises because all creative ideas that work are always, by definition, logical in hindsight. People then assume that, since they are logical in hindsight, the way to generate them is by ploughing through logic. This simply isn't the case: an imaginative leap is still needed.

Consider the following problem.

Add up all the numbers 1 to 100. What's the answer?
There are several ways to do this. Write them down and do simple though lengthy additions; use a calculator; use a computer.

But look at the solution on page 96. It is simple, imaginative, quick and probably the best way to add up these numbers. You'll wish you'd thought of it. It was first developed by Gauss as an answer to the question posed to him in a classroom.

The point is, it is logical in hindsight. In fact, it's so logical, it's obvious. But it took imagination to create it.

All great imaginative ideas that work are logical in hindsight or they wouldn't work. And so we are tempted to think that, if we had thought about it long enough, logically we would have come up with the answer. It's only a question of time and effort and we'd have got there. That may be so, but it's unlikely. A far more powerful approach is to assume that there may be techniques to help us make the imaginative leap that is needed, rather than laboriously trying to get there by working through an infinity of logical permutations.

Trap 2: Brainstorming as the solution

This second trap is at the other end of the spectrum. We decide not to try to get to a solution by working it out logically, but then move to the other extreme by going immediately to a brainstorming exercise.

Brainstorming is by no means the most effective way to get imaginative ideas that work. But it's the only technique that many people have heard of so they use it. And the problem is that, because it often isn't productive in producing ideas that are immediately applicable, the mistaken conclusion is that creative thinking isn't productive and we might as well go back to logic as usual.

Brainstorming then gets the reputation of being a sideshow, fun activity, producing wild thinking that doesn't go anywhere. Moreover, because it's easy it is treated more like a game for relaxation than a method for achieving breakthrough results.

The solution: thinking strategies

The real way to get the sort of creative thinking that gets breakthrough results is not by ploughing through logic, nor by brainstorming.

The thinking strategies explained in this book can be applied as a normal part of doing business, as a mainstream activity. The strategies that work fall into two main types:

➤ Strategies to escape the limitations and boundaries of the left-brained, logic-only approach.
➤ Strategies that help access the right brain, where imagination lies.

For the rest of this chapter, we'll focus on the first type of strategy, some ways to escape boundaries of left-brained logic. Chapter 8 deals with the second type of strategy.

ANSWER: NUMBERS 1 TO 100

Write down the numbers 1 to 50 one way. Write down the numbers 51 to 100 in reverse order underneath. Then add them:

1	2	...	49	50
100	99	...	52	51
101	101		101	101

The answer is clearly $50 \times 101 = 5050$. It's simple when you know how!

Of course, there's hardly ever only one possibility. A creative interpretation of the instruction: 'Add up all the numbers 1 to 100' could be 103 – adding, literally, 1, 2, 100!

Play with boundaries vs play within boundaries

This is an everyday thinking strategy that will help produce the sort of breakthrough results you are after. Simply spend time actively playing with the boundaries of your assumptions. Don't take boundaries for granted. Move them and consider the options that gives you.

PLAY WITH BOUNDARIES

VS

PLAY WITHIN BOUNDARIES

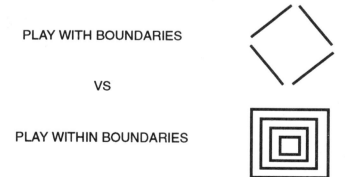

Playing *with* boundaries is very different to allowing the assumption that you'll always want to play *within* boundaries. When you do the latter, what happens also is that people working with you or for you play within tighter and tighter boundaries – because they are not sure where your boundaries are and don't want to risk crossing them.

An example: pricing

Consider how you might price a typical product on the supermarket shelves. Assume that your profits are very poor and your objective, as manager of the business, is to get the maximum price consistent with good volume growth. You want to consider increasing price. However, most organizations are risk averse on this, because of the justifiable fear that increasing price would lose business.

Identify the real or imagined boundaries the organization is assuming as it considers whether or not to increase price. Once you've identified the assumed boundaries, you can make a decision about whether to play with them or not. These are some potential boundaries:

Line pricing

This boundary assumes that several variants of a product need to be at the same price point. It's far easier if everything on a feature or display is at the same price.

However, that's a boundary that restricts how high you can price individual items. Shouldn't a toothpaste that combines three benefits in one, and is more costly to make because of the extra ingredients, be priced higher than the variant that just provides one? Shouldn't the variant of the cosmetic shampoo that also has anti-dandruff ingredients be priced higher than the others?

Large discounts for large sizes

This boundary assumes a rule about the savings consumers want for buying the largest size. But often the consumer gets other benefits from buying a large size and this may be where a price increase could be acceptable. The other consumer advantages could be fewer trips to the supermarket, less time spent in the checkout line, less petrol etc.

Consider a petrol station. One petrol station allows cars only to fill their tanks half full. The petrol station next door allows cars to take a full tank. Which can charge a higher amount per liter or per gallon of petrol?

Alternatively, think about the fact that four seats in a row at a good show can be sold at a higher price per seat than individual seats. Or take a restaurant cover charge for parties of 12 or more that isn't charged for a couple.

So if you can make it a big and valuable convenience for the consumer to buy in bulk, there is no reason that you can't price for it.

Use this example to play with the assumed boundary of needing large price discounts on large sizes.

Comparative price per gram

This boundary is to assume that the consumer is most interested in comparative price per gram between brands. However, using weight or even volume as the basis of comparison is an unreal boundary. Compare concentrated dishwashing liquids to more diluted ones or a soap that melts to a bar that stays firm and lasts. What matters is overall value to the consumer.

Identifying boundaries and playing with them rather than within them can help identify areas where it might be possible to take pricing action while retaining good consumer value and so help keep the business growing.

Think out of the box

Playing with boundaries is sometimes expressed as thinking out of the box. The two concepts address the same issue – the need to escape some of the self-imposed thinking limitations of our left brain. Consider the following mind-opening practice.

MIND-OPENING PRACTICE

Which of the following numbers is most unlike the others?

1   Thirty-one
2   Thirteen
3   One-third

Please make a choice now. Take the time to decide which you would consider most unlike the others. Make a personal choice, here, before moving on. Make a decision, say it out loud in your mind and write it here:

Answer ————————————

ANSWER: MIND-OPENING PRACTICE

Some people choose thirty-one. Some people choose thirteen. Many choose one-third.

And there are logical reasons for each choice. Indeed, you can invent creative reasons for each one being the right answer.

But did you even consider, let alone choose, the number 2? This, after all, is the only number in the exercise which doesn't contain a one or a three.

Did you simply draw an imaginary box round the problem and having done so fail to think your way out of the box?

1	Thirty-one
2	Thirteen
3	One-third

Thinking out of the box will help you identify the figure 2 as a potential option and to consider the problem within the following boundaries, which generate six alternatives to choose from:

1	Thirty-one
2	Thirteen
3	One-third

Don't assume any boundaries which are restricting, especially if they are not there. Creative thinking gets the sort of answer: 'Oh, I didn't realize you were allowed to do that.'

Barriers to thinking out of the box

There are three systemic barriers that stop people thinking out of the box and each of these is solvable.

The first barrier is that in the past thinking out of the box may have been associated only with very wild ideas that didn't seem to go anywhere, or only with brainstorming, so it is not seen as helpful. Below are 10 tips on how to keep this strategy focused on areas where it can help generate breakthrough results.

The second barrier is that thinking out of the box seems to get in the way of action. And we're paid to do rather than think. Action brings results. Too much time spent thinking out of the box is thought of as dithering, so it isn't done. This is such a strong limiting mindset that a later strategy is designed specifically to address it: act in the action zone versus act without thinking.

A third barrier is that the balance of risk and reward in the organization discourages thinking out of the box. This is also addressed below.

10 tips to maximize the results of thinking out of the box

1 Think out of the box proactively as well as reactively
2 Think out of the box about your goals
3 Think out of the box on the scope you're tackling
4 Get tacit knowledge holders to think out of the box
5 Identify the sides of the box
6 Break rote thinking to think out of the box
7 Think out of successful boxes
8 Risk it out of the box
9 Build on it out of the box
10 Sleep on it out of the box

Think out of the box proactively as well as reactively

It is one thing to think out of the box so you can develop alternatives to solve a particular problem – and it can be very useful. But it is often of significantly higher value to think out of the box when you are not faced with a problem, when you are just faced with the present and the future. What do you want the future to look like?

Take time out to think and question some of the barriers and assumptions that are stopping you and the organization from taking action that would get brilliant results. Identify boxes that are constricting you on important issues. Do some possibility thinking. Work *on* the system instead of *in* the system.

This sort of thinking starts with a fresh sheet of paper. It refuses just to accept an improvement on the current approach – and recognizes that a restart is better. Don't be trapped in the box of history.

Using mind-map techniques will also help (see Chapter 9). Don't spend your whole time reacting to other people's bits of paper or e-mails. Start with a fresh sheet of paper and be proactive in your thinking.

PROACTIVE THINKING

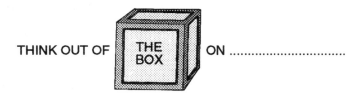

Think out of the box about your goals

It's your choice. No one else's. Don't get boxed into thinking only about the things you have habitually done. Are you thinking and reviewing the right goal area? Are you trying to solve a problem on how to get more sales – because that's what the meeting is for – when you could be better focused on cost? Don't get boxed in by bureaucratic or burden-of-habit boxes, deciding what to think about by default.

Even if you have the right goal area, are you being boxed in by a previously set goal? Remember how often you changed what you wanted to be when you grew up. Are the goals you've set still the right ones? Don't carry on climbing a ladder without checking it's on the right wall.

> It's certainly true that: 'If you don't know where you're going, you'll end up someplace else.'
> But it's also true that: 'If you always know exactly where you're going, you have no chance of discovering someplace else.'

Don't let your goals become rigid boxes. Once in a while, think out of the box of your proclaimed goals to check they are still the best ones. Don't stay with them just because you've declared them.

It's not being unfaithful or indecisive to reconsider goals. Either they need changing or they don't. If they do, do it. If they don't, your period of reconsideration makes you even more powerful and energized in your renewed commitment to them.

Be prepared to think out of the box about what you think about. Make sure that you focus your thinking on the things that will make the biggest difference to breakthrough results. Don't waste your time and talent doing problem solving on incremental minor issues.

Think out of the box on the scope you're tackling

Don't get boxed into dealing with a problem the same way you always have or the same way others have. Make sure you work on the biggest scope you can. This is a really good short cut to breakthrough results. If the problem has happened before, don't focus on how to solve it — but on how to stop it happening again.

Rather than thinking out of the box on a problem, think out of the box about why *you* are spending your time and talent on it. Should it really be you doing it – or should it be someone else? Should the task be delegated?

Continually think about the purpose of the purpose of what you are trying to solve and get to the highest scope you can. Think out of the box with an end in mind and make that the biggest, most meaningful end you can work on.

Get tacit knowledge holders to think out of the box

This is real power. As we have seen, it is the combination of knowledge with creative thinking that gets breakthrough results. The key people to get thinking out of the box are the knowledge holders – because then there is a far, far bigger chance of coming up with ideas, strategies and plans that can be made to work. If a creative idea can be leveraged against high knowledge, it has a good chance of a beneficial result, often a very financially attractive one.

For tacit knowledge holders, one quality idea outside the box sometimes has more power than 20 within the box.

FOR THOSE WITH TACIT KNOWLEDGE...

ONE IDEA OUT OF THE BOX = 20 IDEAS IN THE BOX

Consider the business of baby diapers. All manufacturers used to compete within the traditional box of trying to provide a benefit to mother and child through better and better dryness and leakage prevention with the conventional diaper.

Then someone in Japan with high tacit knowledge of the situations in which mothers put diapers on babies thought out of that box. He realized that changing diapers was still a stress situation for older babies: with the conventional diaper they had to be laid on their backs which they often didn't want and so they struggled.

So he conceived of a diaper for older babies that could be changed with the baby standing up, leaning on its mother's shoulder – called a pull-up.

An out-of-the-box idea to give a benefit to mother and baby that took over the market.

Identify the sides of the box

Identify exactly what the boundaries are that you are accepting when you think about an issue. Search for them. Realize them. Specify them. Write them down. Then decide whether you need to, or are prepared to, accept them.

Break rote thinking to think out of the box

Rote thinking occurs when the whole organization thinks parrot fashion, simply repeating rules and accepted truths.

Senior managers can help generate out-of-the-box thinking by simply removing one of the accepted restrictions that form the boundaries of the box. This then encourages the total organization to break that piece of rote thinking and gets them out of the box.

For example, there may be an assumption with the organization that all projects or ideas have to pass a certain research technique test before they become valid. The organization focuses on ways to pass that particular test. Remove that assumption and you release people to focus on developing ideas that they think will work in the marketplace.

Think out of successful boxes

This is a very rich area of opportunities for breakthrough results. Most people and organizations who believe themselves to have been reasonably successful in their past will probably have developed a high number of assumed rules of what works. These have been successful and so it is difficult to recommend going against the grain.

In these circumstances, knowledge can be quite high but its power is used to reinforce old mindsets and old rules – to support the status quo and rely on incremental improvement.

In such situations, thinking out of the box can be very rewarding. The benefit from and opportunity for thinking out of the box are high because the organization is full of small boxes that constrain people's thinking.

Risk it out of the box

You need to make it low risk to offer an out-of-the-box idea. Ideally you need to make it more risky, when you're looking for breakthrough, to only volunteer in-the-box ideas. You need to provide a juicy carrot for out-of-the-box thinking and a crippling stick for only in-the-box thinking.

Consider the following analogy.

WALKING ON A BEAM: CARROT AND STICK

Imagine a 4 inch wide beam, about 12 feet long. Lay it on the floor. Ask someone to walk along it without falling off. Most people would certainly be prepared to give it a try and no one would fall off. There's not much risk in trying it, nor much benefit in achieving it.

Then put the beam several hundred feet in the air between two tall buildings and ask people to walk across. Most wouldn't try: the consequences of falling off are too great.

Now offer people £100 if they succeed in walking the beam between the buildings. Some would try, most not. Offer £1000. Then £10,000. At some level of potential reward most would try.

And certainly, if you provided a safety net to avoid bad consequences if you fell off, the reward you'd need before you had a go would come tumbling down.

Make it part of everyone's evaluation to list the out-of-the-box thoughts they've come up with, whether or not they worked. In other words, make it part of their evaluation to have a number of 'smart misses'.

Build on it out of the box

Any new idea is by definition a combination of at least two other ideas. If the thought is exactly the same as one you've just had, it cannot be new. If it's new, it must have come from a combination of other ideas. Any thought can be built on to produce a further idea. So half-ideas are valuable: they can be built on.

Moreover, it's unlikely you're going to get it absolutely right first time out of the box. If at first you don't succeed, try, try and try again. So applaud and value half-good ideas and aim to build on them.

Sleep on it out of the box

Don't feel you have to get to every good idea straight away. It's amazing how ideas can mature in the mind if you let it ponder on a problem, consciously or subconsciously. Consider how often you say:

➤ Let me mull it over
➤ Let's sleep on it
➤ Let's do something else and come back to it
➤ Let's turn it over in our minds
➤ Let me ponder it for a bit.

Before you go further, make sure you have tried the following mind-opening practice. Take the time to consider all seven questions thoroughly. You'll get most benefit from this exercise if you also write down all the options you've considered for each question. Only after you've done this look at the solutions.

MIND-OPENING PRACTICE: THINKING OUT OF THE BOX

Try all these questions before looking at the solutions. For best results, write down all the options you consider before looking at the solutions.

1 The numbers exercise

How do you turn VI into seven by adding one line? The answer is to add a line and make VII, the Roman numeral for seven.

How do you turn IX into six by adding one line?

2 The letters exercise

Cross out six letters from the following sequence, so that the remaining letters, without altering their sequence, spell a well-known word:

BSIANXLAETNTAERS

3 The glasses exercise

There are three empty glasses next to three full glasses. By moving just one glass, how could you arrange the glasses such that no empty glass is next to an empty one and no full one next to a full one?

4 Series

What's the next letter in this series?

WTNLIT

5 Eleven

The matches below signify the number six. Add just three matches to equal eleven.

6 Counters

Consider the following arrangement of counters. Move one counter only to end up with two lines each containing four counters.

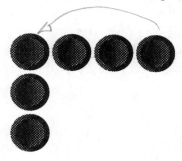

7 Swimming pool

A man has a swimming pool in his garden situated between four splendid oak trees, as shown below:

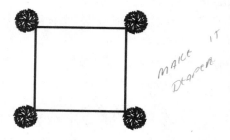

He is rather disappointed with the size of the pool and wants to double its size but keep it square. On the other hand, he doesn't want to cut down any of the oak trees. Can it be done?

ANSWERS TO MIND–OPENING PRACTICE

1 The numbers exercise

i) Add a single curved line to make it SIX.
ii) An alternative is to put a horizontal line through and invert it.

$$IX \quad = \quad \frac{VI}{\Lambda I} \quad \checkmark$$

2 The letters exercise

i) One answer is BANANA. You get it by removing the letters SIX
    LETTERS from the sequence.
ii) Another answer is LETTER. You get it by choosing six letters
    and removing them each time they appear in the sequence. By
    choosing XIANBS, you end up with the word LETTER.

3 The glasses exercise

Take the middle full glass, pour its contents into the middle empty
glass and return it to its place.

4 Series

The answer is 'S'. The letters are the first letters of the words in
the question.

5 Eleven

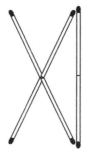

6 Counters

Pick up the end counter in the row of four and place it on top of the counter in the corner, making two rows of four.

7 Swimming pool

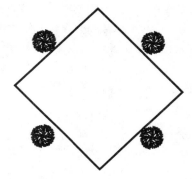

Learning from the mind-opening practice

These examples represent out-of-the-box thinking. In most cases, the solution required you to remove a boundary to the thinking that the box initially assumed. They required you to go beyond the box of limiting assumptions or break out of the limiting rules you assume on how the problem should be tackled.

In the numbers exercise, the pattern was deliberately set up so you would think in the box of Roman numerals. One solution was out of that box. Think outside that box and the solution is relatively easy. The difficult bit is to get outside the box.

In the letters exercise, the box is thinking that six individual letters need crossing out and only six. Within that box, the problem is unsolvable. Think outside the box and other alternatives appear, such as crossing out SIX LETTERS, or six individual letters, each crossed out each time they appear.

In the glasses exercise, the box is thinking that the solution comes from moving the position of any one glass. It should, however, quickly become apparent that thinking in this box will not generate a solution. This may trigger thinking out of the box. The answer lies in moving the contents of one glass, rather than the position of a glass.

In the swimming pool exercise, the box is to maintain the orientation of the pool in the pattern established. In the series exercise, it is thinking that there is a numerical or pattern relationship between the letters themselves. This box is encouraged by previous experience of puzzles. Thinking in this box doesn't generate a solution.

In the eleven exercise, previous patterns also form a box of thinking. The tendency is to think of adding matches to form an equation. Or the experience of the first mind-opener (six) may trigger the alternative of trying to spell the word eleven. But both these are boxes of previous experience. To get the answer you have to think outside of these boxes.

In the counters exercise, the box is to think of moving counters on a flat surface. Previous puzzles might require this. However, you need to think in a different dimension to get the answer.

The box of previous patterns

In several of the above examples, the box to our thinking is caused by previous experience or assumptions based on previous experience.

This is also true in organizational life. It is only by questioning the limitations of such assumptions that we can learn to think out of the box. Question every piece of history, every rule, every 'taken for granted'. However, this is often difficult, particularly if the rule has worked so many times before.

Example

Consider the following organizational problem. The organization is presented with a series of letters and seeks to find a characteristic that is predictable in the future.

P E C H

It finds out that a particular characteristic appears in each letter (✓) or not (x) as follows:

x ✓ x ✓
P E C H

i.e. the characteristic exists in E and H, but not in P and C.

With this experience, someone within the organization may come up with a hypothesis that the characteristic is whether the letter is made up only of straight lines.

Further data comes in on a further two letters as follows:

x ✓ x ✓ ✓ x
P E C H A O

This confirms it and it becomes the accepted belief.

Even further data comes in on other letters:

x ✓ x ✓ ✓ x ✓ x
P E C H A O N S

Now the pattern is very clear: letters made out of straight lines have a tick, those with a curve in are crossed. In 100 percent of the cases tried, this is true. It's a valid rule.

What happens when another two pieces of data come in as follows?

x ✓ x ✓ ✓ x ✓ x x ✓
P E C H A O N S F R

These last two letters don't seem to conform to the pattern! What does the organization do? Typically it will:

➤ double-check the reading on the last two letters – there must be a misprint or a wobble in the research

> ➤ if the research is confirmed, the organization will conclude that the rule is still right, but we just got a couple of rogue recent readings. Up to now it's been 100 percent right. In fact, even if the new data is correct, the rule is still valid in 80 percent of all cases tested and that's more than good enough in the business world. It's not a perfect world.

The problem is that the organization has got itself committed to working in one box; it has become an accepted rule; and it is difficult to go back and challenge it.

In fact, by thinking out of the box and going back over the data, one can see that the ticks are against letters that have a solid base and would stand by themselves; the crosses are by letters that are wobbly due to either a curved base or a single-legged base.

However, the organization has got itself into a limited mindset and forces all new data into that mindset.

> Ours is the age that is proud of machines that think and suspicious of men who try to
>
> H Mumford-Jones

Let's consider how often this happens in a business situation: probably quite frequently in most organizations.

Take an example where an organization is recruiting and has to select one candidate from a final group of eight. Assume that two of the eight aren't available so the choice is between the remaining six.

Eventually, the organization selects one as being the best candidate. Having done so, it gets more and more comfortable with the decision. The mindset is that this is the right person and different people in the organization find all the data to support that conclusion. The selected candidate is introduced around. Everyone is impressed. Everyone finds supporting reasons why this is the right person versus any other candidate.

Then, just before signing the contract, one of the original candidates who wasn't available becomes readily available. And this person would clearly have been the strongest on paper.

Does the organization go back and reevaluate what is the best decision? Or does it carry on with the decision it has already made, even though – in the light of all the information now available – it may not be the right one? Many organizations simply carry on and convince themselves they've made the right decision anyway.

The Fourth Thinking Strategy

Act in the action zone

versus

Act without thinking

6 Acting in the Action Zone

Ideas are cheap and abundant; what is of value is the effective placement of these ideas into situations that develop into action.

Peter Drucker

We have just reviewed the need for creative thinking and several of the other thinking strategies also encourage creative thinking. However, no results, let alone breakthrough results, will come without action.

Many managers will, rightly, get impatient at any approach that isn't geared towards action and making things happen. So it's vital to tackle this issue and explain how these thinking strategies are linked to action. The fourth thinking strategy does that job.

It is of course only action that gets results. But action comes from thinking. All thinking and no action is disastrous, as is all action and no thinking.

The individuals and organizations that will do best will be those that seek to become truly expert at this balance. The secret is not to operate to 'either/or' – it is to operate to 'both'. Think *and* act. Brilliance at understanding how to do both is what produces breakthrough results. Unless this issue of 'how to do both' is addressed up front, an organization will not be able to go beyond the box.

However, many managers feel they are paid to do, rather than think. We often feel we can't afford to waste time creating more options before we decide and act. To do so seems like dithering. Far better to be seen to be decisive and action oriented.

This issue is not a theoretical one. It's real, urgent and very topical. It is currently causing problems for leaders and managers across the board. Consider the words of Dick Brown, chief executive of Cable and Wireless, writing in the *Financial Times* in December 1997:

> *Thinking doesn't change a business, essential as it is. Action changes a business. If I had to choose between high intelligence and effective execution, I would take the effective execution all the time. This is not to disparage the need for creativity and foresight, but unless it is translated into action, it is just a dream.*

Or as Ted Leavitt of the Harvard Business School previously put it: 'Creativity without implementation is irresponsibility.'

These comments emphasize correctly the need for action. However, there is as much interest in the need for thinking.

> *Thinking is work. In the early stages of a man's career, it is very hard work. When a very difficult decision or problem arises, how easy it is after looking at it superficially to give up thinking about it.*
>
> *If I have any advice to pass on as a successful man, it is this: if one wants to be successful, one must think; one must think until it hurts. One must worry a problem in one's mind until it seems there cannot be another aspect of this that hasn't been considered. Believe me, that is hard work and, from my close observation, I can say that there are few people indeed who are prepared to perform this arduous and tiring work.*
>
> *Roy Thomson, Canadian entrepreneur*

How do we solve this dilemma between action and thought, rather than having it as a running sore? You will only get breakthrough results

> Most people don't take the time to
> think. I made an international
> reputation for myself by deciding to
> think twice a week.
> George Bernard Shaw

if it is truly addressed. The way to address it is to set up a working
model within which everyone can work.

A working model for breakthrough results

Act in the action zone

In every situation, there is an optimum balance between taking too
much time to create too many alternatives before moving to action
and not taking enough time to think up alternatives. This balance is
summed up in the contrast between two alternative mindsets:

> Don't just sit there, do something
>
> vs
>
> Look before you leap

Each business situation is different. But for each situation there is an
optimum window between spending too much time creating alternatives and not taking enough time to think of enough alternatives.

In the same way, there is an optimum window for deciding
between the alternatives which you've created, and not doing this too
early or too late.

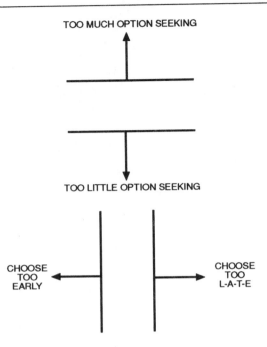

These two windows form an **action zone**. For breakthrough results you need to act within the action zone. Act outside the zone and your results will be poorer, at best incremental.

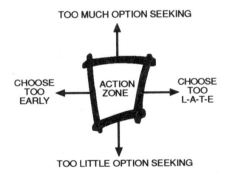

If you act outside the action zone, you'll never get discontinuous, breakthrough results. You'll either not be thinking of enough alternatives or thinking of too many for that situation; or you'll be deciding between the alternatives too early or leaving the decision too late.

Discontinuous results come from staying in the action zone on each major project at each and every stage. They come from continually asking the question: 'Are we in the action zone or are we acting outside of it?'

Each of the four areas outside the action zone spells trouble if you are looking to achieve breakthrough results.

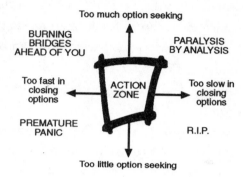

This model was originated by Karl Albrecht in *Brain Power*.

Remember, of course, that the action zone balance of generating the right number of alternatives and how fast you choose between them varies for each different problem and stage of the problem. Each situation has its best action zone. The secret of success is to consistently act in the action zone in a way that is right for each situation.

R.I.P.

This is the trouble area on any situation where you don't spend enough time to generate enough alternatives and then take too long choosing between the few choices you've created. In other words, you don't create enough good options and then you don't even do anything with the limited amount of freedom you've given yourself.

Operate outside of the zone in this area and you and the organization are simply hostages to fortune, victims of circumstance. That's why it's R.I.P. Ultimately you die.

Paralysis by analysis

Otherwise known as paranalysis. This is also never going to get great results and produces incrementalism at best, failure at worst.

In the trouble area of paranalysis you have spent too much effort creating too many alternatives and then spent too long making your mind up between them.

There are situations when there is simply too much choice and the availability of so much choice paralyses decision making. This is true even at the consumer level. Consumers will shy away from making a purchase if the amount of choice available – designed to be to the benefit of the consumer – is actually too big and they are afraid of making a bad choice.

This syndrome can actually be exploited by intermediaries who have the role of simplifying the choice for the consumer. Thus, in the UK, PC World is a chain of stores which specializes in helping the bemused consumer through the vast range of options available for purchasing a personal computer.

Similarly, Carphone Warehouse makes a living by sorting out the huge complexity of options available when buying a mobile phone. Most of the options are relatively cheap, but the sheer variety is so overwhelming that the consumer is likely to 'freeze' and not buy. More choice actually limits the growth of the market rather than expanding it.

Premature panic

This is also a trouble area: not spending enough time creating alternatives and then deciding too fast between the few created. This is a typical area for many action-oriented people and organizations. Their bias for action is so strong that they don't identify those occasions where it's better to pause and think some more to create some better alternatives.

Consider as an example changing pricing in the marketplace. This is an area where there is often premature panic. If sales are disappointing your salesforce may tell you it's because competitors have dropped their prices. You clearly can't afford to let competition buy your business away. And sales are disappointing so you feel you can't simply do nothing.

Your bosses will be asking you what action you're taking. An obvious action is to drop your prices. This will almost certainly cause your sales to strengthen. So you will have appeared to have taken tough action to solve the problem.

However, sometimes this is premature panic. Dropping prices is difficult to reverse and terminally hurts profits, and so you really need to be sure that's the best option. Consider some other alternatives:

➤ Is it a definite fact that competitors have dropped prices? If they haven't, and you drop yours, you will be starting a profit-eliminating spiral, not them.

➤ And if they have changed pricing, is it a temporary promotion or a permanent move? Your action should be different, based on whichever it is.

➤ Is there any other explanation for disappointing sales, e.g. a product reason that you should be taking action on that you won't take if you assume the problem is pricing?

➤ And finally, ask yourself what the problem is that you are trying to solve when you drop prices: probably the problem of disappointing sales. Is this the right problem to be tackling? Isn't the problem that declining sales mean declining profit? And are you really going to be more profitable by dropping prices than by holding price and finding other ways to boost sales?

Premature panic is just too common. Moreover, it is as bad an area in suboptimizing results as paralysis by analysis. But it is often mistakenly considered less serious because it at least results in action. However, people or the organization rarely review afterwards whether they wouldn't have been better taking more time and energy to generate some more alternatives before acting. People kid themselves that there isn't enough time, but looking back afterwards there often clearly was – and that time should have been taken.

Burning bridges ahead of you

This fourth trouble area is just as bad. Having generated a good number of alternatives, you still decide between them too soon; when there is no need to nor any advantage in doing so. It may be far better to 'sleep on it', to 'hold your fire' and see what happens.

But a bias for action misleads you and you make the mistake of closing out your options too early. This way you'll never get discontinuous results. You'll miss out on the 'big play'.

Act in the action zone – but on the right problem

The second part of this groundrule is equally as important as the first. Make sure you're acting on the right problem. For breakthrough results, this means both the most powerful description of the problem or opportunity and the biggest scope of the problem you can tackle.

Continuously review whether the problem you are working on in the zone is the right one. Have you got the best identification of the problem or opportunity you are addressing, the one that will give you the most step-change results if you address it?

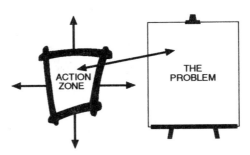

'I'm not returning until you fix it' band leader Count Basie told a club owner whose piano was always out of tune, and he walked out. Some time later the club owner called him to say the piano was fixed and asked if he would return.

Count Basie did, but the piano still sounded awful. 'You told me it was fixed,' he said. 'It is,' said the club owner. 'Can't you see I've painted it?'

Even if you are working in the right problem area, are you working on the biggest scope of problem that will generate the biggest results? Or are you working on symptoms rather than causes? Are you working on the fix that is a big fix, the one that will give step-change results when achieved? Or are you tinkering with the problem, aiming to make incremental improvements that you can celebrate, rather than the big goal towards which you can make discontinuous changes.

Are you working on the level of problem that justifies your talent and energies – or dissipating them on relative minutiae?

Continually review whether the problem or opportunity you are working on in the action zone is fully in line with the first strategy of picturing a step-change vs celebrate doing a bit better.

Acting in the action zone but on incremental issues is still incrementalism. Acting in the action zone on improvements to tangential issues is a waste of your energy.

Write the right problem in the zone. Zone in on the right problem.

Force yourself to write a description of the exact problem. Don't leave it vague. Ensure that people make a decision on the scope of the problem or opportunity they are trying to tackle. It is not enough just to be sure that you are in the action zone, it has to be the action zone of the right problem.

It is quite easy to slip into the bad habit of deciding action on relatively minor issues. The day is easily filled with meetings on these issues, with notes and memos on them, with follow-up action, with measurement and control. Diaries get filled up by such items. Time gets used up. Talent and energy get used up.

The enemy of great business is great busi-ness.

Eventually people become so busy that they don't have time to focus on bigger issues. They are already on overload. They are so caught up with looking at trees, they never get a chance to look at the wood.

'When you're up to your neck in alligators, it's difficult to remember that the original objective was to drain the swamp.'

We create 'alligators' ourselves by focusing energy and talent on relatively minor problems which then create action and programs that have a life of their own. Things can get so bad that people have to go 'off-site' to get any quality time to do any quality thinking. And it's amazing the different perspective, thinking and action that result from a couple of days off-site.

All these problems arise from not insisting on dealing with the biggest scope of problem or opportunity in the action zone, from considering how to treat symptoms instead of how to remove causes, from short-term fixes instead of longer-term solutions, from majoring in minor matters instead of focusing on major matters.

So insist on the value of: 'Write the right problem in the zone. Zone in on the right problem.'

Act in the action zone, on the right problem: a personal case history

In the mid-1980s, I took over the P&G subsidiary in Taiwan, a fledgling business. The origins of the business had been a joint venture formed with a Taiwanese consumer goods company. The brands we operated were a collection of brands that P&G had previously imported into Taiwan, added to the brands that the local Taiwanese company had marketed. However, the subsidiary was not doing well. It was neither big nor profitable; indeed it was losing money.

Action was undoubtedly needed. And that's what I was there for. A fast review of the brands revealed that the volume and profit of almost all of them could be, and needed to be, improved. Our dishwashing business was very weak and not profitable. The toilet soaps shares could be a lot better and their profitability improved. The disposable diaper business was underdeveloped, as was the sanitary napkin business.

The organization – and my boss – were expecting me, as the new head, to take action to fix things.

However, we took the time to consider the right problem in the action zone to work on. We could certainly work on improving what we had and making the current brands we had better.

Indeed, the biggest temptation was immediately to come up with all sorts of ideas and action plans that could be put into operation at once to improve the current business. The organization would respond and get motivated at taking action to improve the brands and their results, versus where they had been. Given that the overall business was in trouble, urgent action was surely needed.

But a quick review showed that wouldn't transform us from a relatively small and unprofitable business into a big, profitable one.

We decided that the right problem to work on wasn't making the most out of what we had. It was to work on the problem of developing a big profitable business in Taiwan.

This caused us to consider all the alternatives. What businesses and brands could we be in and win on in Taiwan that we weren't in already? This drove a study of where competition was very strong and where it wasn't. It drove a study of consumer trends in Taiwan and the outlook over the next five or ten years.

And while we studied, we didn't commit to investment on our current business. We kept options open.

We didn't rush to premature panic or burn our bridges. Nor was it paralysis by analysis. It was just right, in the action zone.

The conclusions from examining the options to solving the 'right problem' were dramatic both in terms of what to do and the speed with which to do it.

The key category in which we could build a big business was

shampoos. The market was big and growing. The Taiwanese, particularly the young, were accepting western brands in all categories, often paying premium prices for premium-quality products. Yet, at that time, Taiwan's shampoo market was still full of low-priced, lower-quality local brands. No multinational company had yet focused on shampoos.

By contrast, in other categories, multinationals had acquired or established strong, 'impregnable' share positions ahead of us – for example, in laundry products or toilet soaps.

The key action was to focus on establishing a big shampoo business and, moreover, to take action fast while there was a window of opportunity, before competition got established in this category too.

By contrast, focusing on the existing dishwashing or toilet soap business was not going to result in a big, profitable business, and anyway could wait its turn for attention. Nothing much was going to change.

The subsidiary focused on getting four shampoo brands into the market fast, with a bias for quick action versus a lot of testing.

Not only did this succeed in building a big, profitable Taiwan subsidiary, the action also produced successes that would subsequently be successful around the world. The Taiwan subsidiary was the first outside the US to introduce a 2-in-1 shampoo, later to become Wash & Go and which traveled the world; the subsidiary also resurrected the Pantene brand, subsequently expanded around the world.

Here is an example for you to practice acting in the action zone, on the right problem.

EXAMPLE: WIDGETS

Consider the following data and suggest action.

Your company produces widgets, under your own trademark and sold to retailers nationally. Your sales have declined somewhat and your plant is operating at only 50 percent capacity. At this point you are at break even.

The variable or direct cost of your widgets is £4. Your cost including overheads is £5. The selling price to retailers is £6.

A major retailer approaches you to ask you to supply them with a large order and put the store's own-label trademark on the widget. The retailer would pay £4.50 for each unit, which wouldn't cover the full cost but would more than cover the direct cost, make a good contribution to your overheads and put you in profit.

What action would you take?

Decide what you would do before reading the solution overleaf.

You can easily see from this exercise that the actions you came up with were a direct result of how you defined the scope of problem. Define the problem in the way that is most likely to give you discontinuous results. In the above example, all but the last approach will yield incremental improvements at best, which will not be sustainable.

MIND-OPENING PRACTICE: ACT IN THE ACTION ZONE

You are in a group captured by cannibals. The cannibals are shortly going to have lunch. As pre-lunch entertainment, they give you two sandtimers, one for 7 minutes, one for 4 minutes. The chief says that you will be spared from being cooked if you can tell him exactly when 9 minutes have elapsed, starting from now. What do you do?

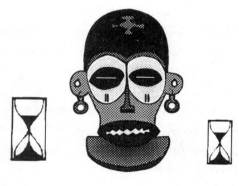

WIDGETS: THE SOLUTION

The action you decide to take depends directly on how you define the scope of the problem and the sort of results you are seeking.

There are several different levels of problem you can tackle.

How to make a profit this year? If this is what you are after, you would probably decide on the action to accept the order.

How to maximize profits this year? You might then decide on two actions: (a) accept this order and (b) seek similar offers from other retailers until your plant is at full capacity.

How to fix the business to become sustainably profitable? You might then decide, instead of considering the retailer's order, to attack your costs – to decrease both direct and indirect costs so that you become sustainably profitable at a lower level of sales. This might even involve taking a short-term hit in restructuring charges in order to fix the basics. If you defined the scope this way, you might turn down the retailer's order – at least for the time being, until you'd had a chance to review the option of restructuring your costs.

This definition of the problem would throw up an alternative approach: how to reverse the declining sales trend. What are the options for doing so – better marketing; more investment in advertising; broader sales coverage; inventing an improved widget; inventing such an improved widget that you could sell at higher prices?

How to make step-change profits over the medium term? Under this definition of the scope yet different options emerge. The declining sales of your widget suggest a fundamental issue. Moreover, the retailer could go elsewhere to get an own-label widget at any stage in the future. The retailer's sales of its own widget will eat into your sales anyway. Are you really in a business that still allows you to get great profit results in the future? Is there another product line you can or should move to, given your plant and core competencies?

ACT IN THE ACTION ZONE: ANSWER TO MIND-OPENING PRACTICE

The action zone for this problem is clear. And you have probably committed yourself to death by not acting at once. You are literally in 'R.I.P.' trouble, not just paranalysis. You cannot sit back and think how to solve the problem. As soon as you start thinking without doing anything, you lose all your reference points on time and so consign yourself to death.

The action to take is immediately to turn over the timers. The only decision is to whether to turn over one or both. Then you have time to think what to do next.

Choose to turn over both, immediately. There is no risk to this. You can always reverse one of them within the next minute or so without any loss of flexibility.

Now you have time to think. You have bought time.

The next decision point will come when the 4-minute timer is half finished and it's too late to reverse it without loss of flexibility.

Assume you let the 4-minute one run its course. What would you then do?

Assume you'll turn it back over. The next decision would then come when the 7-minute one is finished.

Assume you would turn that over. When the 4-minute timer is finished (and therefore 8 minutes will have passed) there will be one minute's worth of sand in the bottom of the 7-minute one. Turn that over to make 9 minutes.

This mind-opener is a good illustration of an occasion when it is best to take some action, buy time to think and then adjust the plan again once you've thought more or know more.

MIND-OPENING PRACTICE: ACT IN THE ACTION ZONE

Consider:

Opportunity ISNOWHERE

Think about this, then read the comments on page 132.

'OPPORTUNITY': ANSWER TO MIND-OPENING PRACTICE

A typical response to this stimulus is to make sense of the misprint by interpreting it as:

Opportunity IS NOWHERE

But this is a very limiting interpretation that doesn't seem in keeping with how we want to view the present or the future. Typically we accept and act on the first interpretation that makes even limited sense, even if it's not the only or even best interpretation.

A minute spent generating alternative options would yield:

Opportunity IS NOW HERE

We frequently get into situations covered by the action-zone trouble areas. Consider how often you hear phrases like:

➤ 'A bird in the hand is worth two in the bush.' This drives a mindset of closing down options. Adopting it broadly, in too many situations, will push you to premature panic and burning bridges ahead of you. It won't lead to breakthrough results.

➤ 'Beggars can't be choosers.' This drives a reluctant acceptance that you have no more than one option. Adopted too broadly, this will push you towards premature panic and business collapse.

➤ 'Hobson's choice.' This describes not liking either of two options. Again, too often in this area and you are nowhere near breakthrough results.

➤ 'Any action is better than no action.' This drives an early decision between early options.

➤ 'We backed the wrong horse.' We chose the wrong option.

➤ 'We jumped on the wrong train' or 'We jumped into it too early.' These describe closing down an option too early.

➤ 'Look before you leap.' This encourages avoidance of premature panic or burning bridges.

➤ 'We missed the train.' This describes deciding too late.

The richness and frequency of these phrases show how often the action zone is relevant to your decision making and how often people are suboptimizing their performance in it. That's why they are getting at best incremental improvements, rather than breakthrough results.

Deciding fast on some problems

One response from individuals and organizations is that some problems don't merit acting in the action zone, taking time to consider whether there are enough alternatives or whether you're choosing between them too early.

There are two responses to this. The first is that it is amazing how often just a little thought would have created a better solution. 'If I'd taken a second to think about it, I'd have ...', 'I didn't give it a minute's thought, only to find out later ...', 'I didn't take time to think it through ...' are all frequently heard.

The reality is that it only takes a minute to give it a minute's thought. A minute is quite a long time. Remember how long a minute's silence seems to go on for. Too often, however, particularly in meetings, we give a problem an hour's discussion without ever giving it a minute's thought.

The second response is even more pertinent to getting breakthrough results: if problems come to you that do not merit thinking about then you're spending time on the wrong problems – it's likely you haven't delegated enough or don't have the right operating structure. The right problem you should be focused on is how to avoid being involved in problems that aren't worth thinking about.

Put differently, if you and the organization don't find it useful to act in the action zone, on the right problem then, by definition, you are focused on minor things and are destined at best to improve incrementally on the status quo, never achieving breakthrough results.

The Fifth
Thinking Strategy

Become a
whole-brained

versus

Half-brained organization

7 *Becoming Whole-Brained*

The left side of the brain has dominated strategy formulation, with its emphasis on logic and analysis. Overly structured, this creates a narrow range of options. Alternatives which do not fit into the predetermined structure are ignored. The right side of the brain needs to become part of the process with its emphasis on intuition and creativity.

Mintzberg

This strategy will make a huge difference in achieving breakthrough results. Moreover, the techniques for becoming whole-brained are relatively easy and we already do some of them by instinct. The opportunity is to find a way to apply them systematically and thoroughly to everything we do.

The issue, however, is that many individuals and organizations have picked up habits and procedures that keep them trapped in left-brained-only thinking. Continuing these habits, and not adopting new ones, will leave them limited in exploiting the full power of their brains. It will leave them programmed to do only incrementally better than history – with no real chance of getting breakthrough results.

Becoming whole-brained is no more than learning to use the full power of the brains we have been given and the brains we have hired.

What are the lowest cost, highest powered, non-linear computer systems that can be mass-produced by unskilled labor?
NASA

The brains we have, and the brains we hire, are cranial computers. Yet in your organization:

➤ How many people know how to use a personal computer but don't know how to use their own cranial computer?

➤ How many people know about the latest software for their laptop computer but don't have a clue about the latest software for their cranial computer?

➤ How many people can now surf the Net but don't know how to blow their mind?

The techniques to become whole-brained are no more than very simple software for your mind. Yet many people continue to use old, outdated cranial software out of habit – when for their personal computer they would insist on access to the very latest software.

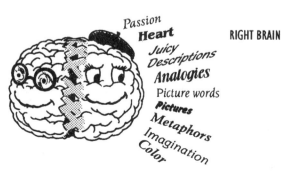

LEFT BRAIN
Logic
Lists
Numbers
Analysis
Linear
Head
Logic
Lists
Numbers
Analysis
Linear
Head
1234567890

Passion
Heart
Juicy Descriptions
Analogies
Picture words
Pictures
Metaphors
Imagination
Color

RIGHT BRAIN

The theory of becoming whole-brained

This strategy is based not just on logic but on something even stronger – science. And on science that got a Nobel prize. That should be recommendation enough for any sceptic.

You will probably have heard of the scientific research started in the early 1980s by Sperry and Ormstein. In summary, they showed clearly that there are two halves to the brain that carry out different processes. The left half, the logical half, deals with words, numbers, logic, analysis, lists and sequencing.

The right half, the so-called creative half, deals with pictures, rhythm, color, imagination, daydreaming and spatial awareness.

Many western organizations have over time become almost only left-brained because that was the way to win.

The issue, however, is that imagination is located in the right half of the brain, the opposite half to logic. To get to creative thinking we need imagination, so we need to gain access to the right half of the brain. Moreover, to get the passion and power behind achieving breakthrough results, we need to find a way to access the right half as well as the rationale of the left half.

More and more scientific evidence is emerging that the power of our brains is only unleashed if we find a way to use both halves of the brain in harmony. Typically this is the way we used our brains up until about 7 or 8 years old. That period for each of us was by far the fastest learning curve in our lives. We combined color and pictures and touch and rhyme with numbers and words and lists and, as a result, learnt more in four years than we subsequently did in the next 20.

An analogy: the basketball match

Take the analogy of a basketball match. On one side you have a team of players using only their left foot, left arm and left eye. They are playing a team using both feet, both arms, both eyes.

Imagine it. If the first team scores 5 points in the match, how many points do you think the team using both arms and both legs would score? 50? 100? The point is that it is far more than double. Using both increases their power by a factor more like 10 or 100.

	TEAM A	VS	TEAM B
USE	One leg only		Both legs
	One arm only		Both arms
	One eye only		Both eyes
SCORE	5	VS	?

It is the same with the left and right brains. You release incredible power if your organization can start to learn to use both. It's not either/or – it's both.

Of course, this concept is not really new. It just needs to be expanded and made systemic. Organizations already have sporadic successful experience of the model of using both the left and right brain. For example:

➤ In media, people quickly moved from radio to television. Television, with pictures, excites the right brain, while the left-brained logic of the argument is maintained. Indeed, the most successful radio advertising conjures up pictures and drama in the consumers' heads – a right-brained activity – rather than relying on words alone – a left-brained activity. Television then moved from left-brained black and white to include color that essentially excites the right brain.

➤ In advertisements, people aim to appeal to both the head (left brain) and the heart (right brain). They are seldom successful if they appeal only to one.

➤ In business presentations, people now use visuals and color – exciting the right brain – rather than relying on a written memo or reading a script, often left-brained only.

➤ In a sales operation, people interact with customers and use both left-brained argument and right-brained visuals and demonstrations. People know they will not succeed just by sending a formal written recommendation to customers.

➤ In public relations, people do better with a holistic approach involving emotion, analogy and metaphors – right-brained concepts – than if they just supply 'logic–only' position statements and questions/answers that are left-brained only. Beyond this, left-brained logic alone is often inadequate to convince third parties, associations or consumer groups, who see things differently; you need to appeal to their emotions to get them to see the data in your way.

➤ In business decisions, experienced managers successfully add right-brained judgement, opinion and gut feel to go alongside strictly left-brained logic and analyses.

Whole-brained versus half-brained

The concept of left brain and right brain is not new. What is new is the science behind this expression and, based on this, the easy techniques we can use to access both the left and the right brain at will. Psychologists throughout history have noticed the difference between convergent thinking (left brain) and divergent thinking (right brain).

In Oriental cultures, there is the concept of yang (left brain) as distinct from yin (right brain).

Freud distinguished between a set of primary functions (left brain) and secondary functions (right brain).

Jung distinguished between the persona (left brain) and the shadow (right brain).

More recently, De Bono distinguished between vertical thinking (left brain) and lateral thinking (right brain).

The opportunity

The opportunity is to drive whole-brained activity throughout everything you do, to replace half-brained activity and so release power to achieve breakthrough goals.

The problem is that, unfortunately, many western-educated people and organizations have drifted into a limiting left-brained-only approach. They are stifled in a restrictive strait-jacket of relentless logic, analysis, colorless script, boring memos, black and white lines of emotionless jargon.

Hours and hours are spent handling in-trays and administration that is all only left brained. And it gets worse as information pollution takes over. Further hours are spent in analyzing data and producing tables and figures. Yet more hours are spent in meetings in left-brained-only discussion and processes.

And all this is done in a context where logic only is praised and admired. Smartness is measured not by the ability to unleash the whole brain, but on the ability to manipulate only part of it – the left part.

Education begins with infants and young children using whole-brained techniques: numbers and rhyme; words and pictures; logic and music; study and play; figures and color. And with these whole-brained techniques young children learn at the speed of light. They learn to walk and talk, to read and write. In learning terms, they grow like weeds.

Then what happens? Because of our habits of history, we decide at about age 7, enough of that, you must grow up. And then instead of books with color and pictures that excite the whole brain we make them read books with no pictures, no color, just black and white print. Instead of playing, we force them to sit up straight and face the front. Instead of thinking things that are fanciful and imaginative, we force them to be sensible.

This represents an addictive, habitual conversion to left-brained-only thinking that has been a huge error.

The age of personal computers is probably, and unexpectedly, beginning to correct this mistake. The software is in color. The graphics are stimulating. Computer games are whole-brained. Young people expect color and image, movement and even music from their computer. This will help reverse the trend towards limited left-brained-only thinking.

But most of our organizations, most of the people within them, most of the habits and practices and procedures, are focused on left-brained-only thinking. Logic rules. Why be given whole brains and not use them? Why hire whole brains and not use them?

We used to measure our assets as 'horsepower'. Then came 'manpower'. This was replaced by 'headcount'. This is right because it recognizes the movement towards hiring heads instead of hands. But the future is not in headcount, it is in brainpower.

HORSEPOWER

TO

MANPOWER

TO

HEADCOUNT

TO

BRAINPOWER

Which is it better to have: organization A with 50 people stuck in limited incrementalism, perversely using only half their brains, bogged down in administering the status quo? Or organization B with 25 people using their whole brain, creative and inspirational, on fire, seeking to achieve the impossible and thrilled by the prospect?

Instinctively, using both gut and logic, you'll probably decide that organization B has more power, even if it has a lower headcount. Indeed, the chances are – given today's downsizing – that organization B will embark on a headcount cut, in part to try to capture the free-spirit feeling of the smaller organization.

The key is to focus not on headcount but on brainpower. And to get the whole organization focused on becoming whole-brained versus half-brained; not just doubling your brainpower, multiplying it by a factor nearer to 50 or 100.

What do you get out of being whole-brained?

If you are whole-brained you add creativity, imagination and passion to logic, analysis and facts. Consider the power that comes from this combination:

Logic   + Creativity
Analysis + Imagination
Facts   + Passion

It isn't either/or. It's both. To get breakthrough results, the individual and the organization need to add creativity to their inherent logic; imaginative thinking to their structured analysis; passion and emotion to their dispassionate facts.

Consider also the power of the whole brain in generating motivation to achieve results. As a simple example, many people feel they ought to lose weight or go on a diet. But few are successful at it. The main reason is that it stays a left-brained, logic-only exercise. It is certainly logical to do it: clearly some weight needs to be lost. But it's difficult and painful to achieve it so little happens. The left-brained-only motivation is inadequate.

The most powerful way to do it is to use the emotions and imagination of the right brain to create energy and motivation to achieve the desired result. Use both the juicy carrot and the crippling stick.

The juicy carrot is the visualization of how you'll look and feel when you've lost weight and how others will feel about you. Imagine the six-pack stomach. Even prepare a photo of yourself with the six-pack stomach. Or imagine the healthy, taut thighs. The slim, non-jowly chin. Imagine beyond that the benefits this will bring: the ability to wear certain clothes, for example. Even invoke the power of your sexual partner — and imagine what things will be like when you're in the shape you'd like to be.

Add to the juicy carrot the crippling stick. Become intensely embarrassed at how you now are and how people might describe you in their minds — a fat slob; letting yourself go; already gone to seed.

Imagine yourself naked and what a sight you are – repulsive.

Using the right brain to generate both a juicy carrot and a crippling stick generates far more motivation than a left-brained-only, logical approach ever does.

As with losing weight, so with many areas of personal and business life. The motivation to achieve something is a factor of 50 or 100 times stronger if it is whole brained.

Those who generate a passion for something are far more likely to get breakthrough results. Those who remain only intellectually committed to something will not have the same power to overcome the inevitable difficulties along the way.

There is hardly a situation you can think of, in stretching for a goal or a result, where the addition of creativity, imagination and passion to the traditional logic, analysis and facts won't produce discontinuously better performance.

LEFT BRAIN	AND	RIGHT BRAIN
Logic		Imagination
Analysis		Passion
Lists		Color
		Pictures
Numbers		Metaphors
		Analogies
Linearity		'Picture' words
		Juicy descriptions

A whole-brained act of persuasion

The following anecdote illustrates the difference between using half-brained thinking and whole-brained thinking to persuade people.

In the late 1980s, I was chairman of the UK Soap and Detergent Industry Association. The issue of the environment was a pressing one and the role of the detergent industry in this respect was coming under question. I was given the opportunity to speak to a group of Conservative MPs over a lunch at the House of Commons and a few weeks later the same opportunity with a group of Labour MPs.

In theory, the speech to the Conservative MPs should have been easier. They were more likely to be sympathetic to the needs and objectives of industry.

But that speech didn't go well. It was essentially a left-brained speech. It was full of facts and figures which illustrated the good work the detergent industry was doing; it explained the good work being done to produce these products with respect for the environment and making the products themselves more and more environmentally friendly.

The speech quoted the mammoth energy savings being made, the packaging and process savings. But it was boring. I lost the attention of the MPs, some of whom started talking among themselves. Moreover, I hadn't really been able to get across the uniqueness of the detergent industry – that its inherent *raison d'être* was linked to a clean environment. And partly as a result of this shortcoming, during the discussion we were continually under attack that no matter how much we were doing, it wasn't enough.

By the time of the lunch for Labour MPs I'd determined to be more whole-brained to illustrate the point of this unique reason for being. The speech started along the following lines:

As you sit before me after lunch, you form a perfect example of what the purpose of the soap and detergent industry is all about. You have sat down at a very clean tablecloth, made so by one of our products, even though yesterday it was stained and dirty. I hope you washed your hands before the meal, and your hands will have been made clean by one of our products. And you'll have done this in a toilet made hygienically clean by one of our products. You have eaten off hygienically clean plates made so by one of our products, even though just a few hours ago they were covered with the germs of others. You have confidently put a fork into your mouth, made hygienically clean by one of our products, even though that very fork was yesterday in the mouth of a diseased Conservative MP. And I hope, like your mother told you, you're wearing clean underwear, made hygienically clean by one of our products. Ladies and gentlemen, the detergent industry is unique. Our very purpose is to provide products to deliver a superbly clean, hygienic environment, and to produce those products in an environmentally caring way.

This introduction engaged the MPs' whole brains. Once that was done, they were receptive to receiving the same facts and figures in support that the previous week had fallen on deaf ears. This was whole-brained persuasion.

MIND-OPENING PRACTICE: BECOME WHOLE-BRAINED VS HALF-BRAINED

What is the maximum number of squares you can see in the picture below?

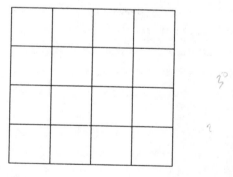

Spend longer on the problem. Assume that you will be given £1 for each square you can see. Now's the time you can secure your future. Think out of the box.

BECOME WHOLE-BRAINED VS HALF-BRAINED:
FIRST SOLUTION TO MIND-OPENING PRACTICE

You don't need to make a decision yet. There is no time limit. You can choose to think of some alternatives. You are asked for the maximum number of squares you can see. Are you sure you have seen as many as possible?

Think further. There is a second answer to this mind-opening practice on page 148.

Remember, you are getting £1 for each square you see.

Eight ways to engage the right brain

It is relatively easy to engage the right brain. The techniques are at our fingertips. Often it seems it is almost a matter of remembering to do so. However, our traditional western practices too often lead us into left-brained-only considerations of logic, analysis and facts.

To get breakthrough results, you need to make it second nature also to engage the right brain, regularly and systematically. Learn habits and practices that automatically switch it on and engage it.

You need to get a feel for the difference between gaining access to your right brain versus staying on the left. Do these exercises quickly:

A (i)   What is the seventh letter of the alphabet?
  (ii) How many days are there in November?
  (iii) Count down the numbers from 26 to O.

B (i)   Write down instructions for getting from your home to your office by car. What is the sequence of left turns and right turns?
  (ii) Write down how to tie a tie or a shoelace.
  (iii) Recite the alphabet backwards.

In the 'A' problems you stay in left-brain mode. Mostly they simply require rote thinking – repeating words, letters or numbers in your mind. It's almost automatic. Even for the days in November, most people don't need to think beyond reciting the rhyme '30 days hath September, April, June and November'.

The 'B' problems should feel different. They trigger access to the right brain. They require you to picture things in your mind (the right brain) and then use the left brain to translate these pictures or movements into instructions.

You are easily able to count down the numbers from 26 to 0 partly because of rote learning and partly because of the logic involved. Only the left brain is needed. But most people can't easily recite the alphabet backwards because it has been learnt by rote one way only and there is no logic. It needs an alternative approach.

Here are eight simple devices to help engage the right brain as well as the left:

1 Use color
2 Use pictures
3 Use metaphors and analogies
4 Appeal to emotion
5 Use your gut feel
6 Use stories as well as data
7 Use picture words as well as jargon
8 Use mindmaps instead of lists and notes

Use color

This is simple but effective. The next time you write something, use different colored pens or different colored paper, including some striking colors. Use different colors to underline, to highlight, for key words or titles, for summations or key phrases.

You will almost feel a certain lightness to your work. It will be more cheerful, more striking, more memorable, more fun.

This is your right brain being engaged. The thoughts that come into your mind will be slightly different. You'll feel less in a box, more out of the box. You will feel unconventional.

After doing this for a few weeks, try reverting to black and white

BECOME WHOLE-BRAINED VS HALF-BRAINED:
SECOND SOLUTION TO MIND-OPENING PRACTICE

You may by now have seen up to 30 squares. The 16 little squares, the 9 squares of two-by-two, the 4 squares of three-by-three and the one big square they are all in.

But why are you satisfied with your answer? Do you assume these are the rules within which to think? You were after all asked for the maximum you could see. Why are you in premature panic to give an answer? You only have £30.

There is a further response to this mind-opening practice on page 150.

---

only. It will seem very boring, dull, routine, trapped in convention and habit.

Color is present in most business communications because technology now allows it. A presentation is made with color slides. Photocopies can be made in color. Personal computers have color graphics. Of course, television and newspapers have long moved to color.

Imagine the opposite. A return to newspapers that are black and white only. Black and white television and films. Black and white slides at business presentations. Computer screens full of data, black on white only.

Everything would seem like hard work to study, watch or read. You'd feel as if you were in a dark pit. This is because the right brain would be deactivated and it would take enormous energy to engage it when faced with a sea of colorless communication.

If this is so clear, why on earth persist with your own single, dull color, out of habit that started with the quill pen? Remember, single color equals single tone, monotone, monotonous, boring.

Use pictures

As with color, so with pictures. A picture really does speak a thousand words. Don't get trapped in the left-brained-only world of columns of figures and facts and pages and pages of words. Television has taken over from radio as the medium of choice. Personal computers have powerful graphics and charts to bring information to life. A business presentation with words on slides is never as effective as one with good visuals. Pictures work because they engage the right brain.

So as you study, write, communicate or plan, use pictures to help engage the right brain. They need not be accurate. They can be very rough; they can be approximate; they can be symbols; they can be simple. But thinking 'What picture would illustrate this?' engages the right brain. And a combination of color and pictures is even better.

Use metaphors and analogies

When you are trying to communicate something, feel free to use metaphors and analogies to get your point across. These are far more powerful than sticking to a dry description of the facts or the intent.

Metaphors and analogies bring the right brain to life, yours and others. They stimulate excitement and involvement. They help paint the picture in a far more powerful way than an emotionless description.

For example, if you have a problem of overlapping roles and responsibilities, a typical action may be to do a survey and analysis of the problem. A more right-brained way of approaching it would be to say 'we have too many cooks spoiling the broth' and agree who is going to cook the broth and who isn't.

By comparing the goal or problem with something else, something in a different frame of reference, metaphors and analogies unblock the constraints of the current situation and current thinking. Once you use a phrase like 'Let's aim to be like Microsoft' or 'Let's be as popular as Coca-Cola is in soft drinks', it breaks the mind out of its current box and releases barriers to your thinking.

Appeal to emotion

There's nothing wrong with emotions. They are real and can be far more powerful than logic. The combination of both is unstoppable.

BECOME WHOLE-BRAINED VS HALF-BRAINED:
THIRD SOLUTION TO MIND-OPENING PRACTICE

Remember the promise was that you would be given £1 for every square you could see. Seeing involves the imagination and the right brain. You can see in this picture whatever you choose.

Up to now you have probably been using the left brain only. You are seeking solutions that are very logical and could be fully justified in a vigorous manner that no one could contradict.

Start gradually to introduce more and more right-brain thinking, more and more imagination.

You could see a square just inside each of the original squares, formed by the inner edge of the line surrounding the square. This is similar to a drawer pulling out of a cabinet – the drawer forms a square just slightly smaller than the hole into which it fits. That's another 30.

You could see a square, a very small one, at each point where the lines cross. That's another 25.

You could see each line as being a series of little squares joined up – make the squares small enough and you are a millionaire.

You could see this picture as being the front face of a Rubik's cube, multiplying all the above numbers by 6.

You could see this picture as an infinitesimally long line of Rubik's cubes going back in a straight line into the paper.

Gradually you are moving from left-brained-only thinking to left and right brained. This opens up new possibilities. They are all valid, just more imaginative. And as you move to add more right-brained ideas, you get richer and richer.

Television advertisements are far more powerful when they appeal to the heart as well as the head. A dry recitation of the facts about a product will hardly ever be effective in getting someone to buy it. When these facts are combined with emotional appeal, the sale is made.

For example, you might have seen the advertisement for tires which emphasizes the role they play in safety using a big picture of a tire with a baby sat in it – logic and emotion combined.

Speeches and presentations are significantly more powerful when they appeal to the audience's emotions as well as to their logic.

As with speeches and advertisements, so with all other forms of thinking and communication. Actively considering the emotions involved – the right brain as well as the logical left brain – generates significantly more powerful results. Do this systematically. Use your own emotions and appeal to the emotions of others.

Use your gut feel

Too often we ask 'What are the facts?' and don't ask 'What's your gut feel?' Facts alone are left-brained. Gut feel alone is right-brained. The combination of the two is all powerful.

Perhaps the biggest decisions any individual makes in their life are whole-brained, not logic only. The three biggest are probably who they marry; what job or career they follow; where they live. They may make such decisions several times in their lives. But, in general, none of these is made just on the basis of logic, analysis and facts.

Who you marry is certainly not an emotionless decision, based only on hard facts and logic. The job or career you take depends a lot on how you feel about it, often on the basis of a few signals, impressions and your sense of affinity for it, as much as on analysis. The house you live in is chosen as much on the basis of your feel for it as on the cold hard facts – indeed, you'll often pay an illogical premium just to live in a place you like.

To achieve discontinuous results, be prepared to employ your gut feel as well as your logic in business as well as in your personal life. Be whole-brained, not half-brained.

Use stories as well as data

'The facts speak for themselves.' How untrue that is. This is often the statement of someone who is falling short of full persuasion.

If the facts did indeed speak for themselves, there would be no debate. Everyone would already have come to the same obvious conclusion. The very fact that you have to point out that 'the facts speak for themselves' means they don't. People are still not persuaded. The job is only half done.

Be prepared instead to use stories and anecdotes to put the facts into perspective – to bring things to life in a way that others can relate to. One story, one example, one anecdote can be more powerful than a pageload of facts, and more memorable too.

For example, perhaps you are trying to convince others of consumers' reaction to your product. You can produce table after table of market research. But there are often different ways to interpret the numbers in a left-brained way, particularly if the issue is not that clear cut. Add to the mix a story of your own interaction with some specific consumers. Relate exactly what they said and the emotion with which they said it. This adds flavor to the dry numbers and facts.

Use picture words as well as jargon

Most jargon is, by nature, left-brained. It is a representation of a set formula. When we use a piece of jargon, it's assumed that everyone knows what we mean. Even worse is to go beyond jargon to abbreviations, to 'management by alphabet'. This, by its nature, is restrictive, highly limiting in its meaning. All of this has a place, but it's not every place.

Instead, if you want to capture a meaning in its fullest sense, don't be afraid to use picture words. These are words that may not even be legitimate in a literal or grammatical sense, but conjure up a picture of the meaning you want. The picture words strike a chord in the right brain.

In this chapter so far you've encountered picture words or groups of picture words such as: 'the facts-speak-for-themselves syndrome', 'management by alphabet', 'whole-brained versus half-brained', 'feel' a certain 'lightness' to your work.

Picture words are like pictures. They engage the right brain in a way that jargon never can.

Use mindmaps instead of lists and notes

Mindmaps are explained in Chapter 9. Essentially they are a systemic way of engaging the right brain. They combine many of the technical elements above, such as pictures, key words and color. They stimulate creativity and use of the imagination. And they stimulate you to use your gut feel in decisions.

Male/female – left/right brain?

The left and right hemispheres of the brain are connected by a chord like a thick fibre called the corpus callosum. What is interesting is that the corpus callosum in females is significantly thicker than that in males. This is scientifically proven.

As yet there is no scientific proof for the possibility that the thicker the connection between left and right brains, the easier it is to move rapidly between them. Or that the thinner the connection, the more difficult it is. If this were right, nevertheless, it would explain some differences in male and female behavior.

The male often had to leave the home for a long time to hunt for food or go to war. He needed to separate out this logical need from his emotions at leaving the family. Over time a thinner corpus callosum helped him do this.

By contrast, the female's thicker corpus callosum would help explain her more frequent use of intuition that rests in the right brain; her ability to switch more rapidly between logic and emotions and back again; and her ability to have conversations that branch off into subtributaries of the main theme as her right brain becomes engaged and new ideas pop into her mind.

But everyone's corpus callosum is plenty thick enough to learn to be able to engage both halves of the brain at will. Become whole-brained instead of half-brained if you want breakthrough results.

The Sixth Thinking Strategy

Choose powerful

versus

Limiting mindsets

8 Choosing Powerful Mindsets

Every manager carries around in his, or her, head a set of biases, assumptions, and presuppositions.

Gary Hamel

All the strategies designed to get breakthrough results will flounder when faced with a strongly held limiting mindset. A limiting mindset can stifle and overcome any of the other actions to stimulate behavior to get breakthrough results. It can be the rock against which all these efforts flounder.

Limiting mindsets form the walls of the box of incrementalism. Without changing the mindset it's impossible to break out of the box.

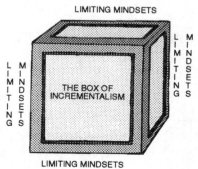

As with all the thinking strategies, both halves of the equation are important. Breakthrough results will come both from getting intensely dissatisfied with limiting mindsets (the crippling stick) and from getting attracted by the benefit of powerful mindsets (the carrot).

It is not enough to learn or adopt a new mindset for the future. For breakthrough results, you need to get rid of the limiting ones you are carrying.

Hamel and Prahalad made this point in *Competing for the Future*:

> *Although much in vogue, creating a learning organization is only half the solution. Just as important is creating an unlearning organization. Why do children learn new skills much faster than adults? Partly because they have less to unlearn. Music teachers and sports coaches put emphasis on the early development of right habits, because they know that learning is easier than unlearning.*
>
> *To create the future, a company must unlearn at least some of its past. We are all familiar with 'the learning curve', but what about 'the forgetting curve'? – the rate at which a company can unlearn those habits that hinder future success. The more successful a company has been, the flatter its forgetting curve.*

And the point is emphasized by Tom Peters in *The Circle of Innovation*:

> *Organizational learning is one of the hottest management topics of the 1990s (some say even beyond). But I say forgetting is far more important. Forgetting is the key activity – the primary activity – these days.*

Faced with the choice between changing one's mind and proving there is no need to do so, almost everyone gets busy on the proof
John Kenneth Galbraith

What is a mindset?

A mindset is a fixed way of looking at things. We all have mindsets, some of them helpful but many of them limiting. People and organizations have mindsets without realizing it.

A mindset is simply the way you set your mind to look at things. Tell your mind to look at things one way and it will notice, find and imagine a whole host of evidence and reasons to support that perception.

Success depends more on how we set our minds than on how good our minds are in the first place. This is true for individuals, for groups and for organizations.

Often, however, we set our minds in a remarkably blinkered way. For example, adopt the mindset 'This is going to be a bad day' and your mind will find all sorts of examples and reasons to support that point of view and cement that mood. By contrast, ask your mind to address the question 'How can we make this a great day?' and it will create great ideas to achieve that.

Adopt a mindset that 'I am undervalued' and your mind will find slights and criticisms where they were never intended. Adopt the mindset 'Headquarters don't know what they're doing' and your mind will find a host of examples to support that view; so much so that, in the future, any idea coming from headquarters may be dismissed out of hand.

Some mindsets can become quite ingrained based on a few pieces of data and your mind subsequently selects the data to support that view. The mindset can range in strength from a judgement to a strongly held opinion all the way to a bias or a prejudice.

There are two key characteristics of limiting mindsets:

➤ It is very easy to adopt a limiting mindset without realizing it.
➤ Once you have a limiting mindset, your mind is very good at spotting only the data that reinforces it.

That is why supposedly very intelligent people, and very smart organizations, can still be extremely limited and can be described by phrases such as:

➤ They have a closed mind on this

➤ They have a very blinkered attitude

➤ They just can't see it

➤ Their heads are in the sand

➤ They have a blind spot on this

➤ They are narrow-minded on this

➤ Their bias is unshakeable

➤ They are turning a deaf ear to it

➤ They can't see the light of day.

MIND-OPENING PRACTICE: CAR CRASH

A father and his son were traveling in a car far, far too fast. They had a terrible head-on crash with a large, heavy truck. Imagine the scene: mangled wreckage everywhere, both badly injured and trapped in the wreckage. Two fire engines and an ambulance came. They decided to pull the boy out first as he was very badly injured. They got him out, put him in the ambulance and rushed him to hospital, sirens blaring. It took 20 minutes through the traffic. At the hospital door they put him on to a trolley and pushed it quickly into a cubicle in the casualty ward. The doctor came tearing down a corridor, coat flapping, opened the curtains of the cubicle and said: 'Oh no, it's Peter, my son.' What had happened?

Consider what explanations there might be, before looking at one answer on page 160.

MIND-OPENING PRACTICE:
WHY DO PET OWNERS LOOK LIKE THEIR PETS?

Have you not noticed how, over time, pet owners tend to look like their pets? Why does that happen? Is it because pet owners, consciously or subconsciously, adopt the mannerisms of their pets? Or is it that the pets adopt the owners' mannerisms?

Have you noticed this syndrome before? If not, for the next few weeks or so, keep your eyes open for it. I guarantee that, before a month is out, you too will have noticed that pet owners look like their pets.

What happens here and why? What is happening is that you are adopting a mindset and your mind will focus on data which supports it. You may not have looked very carefully before at the characteristics of any pet or even any pet owner. But for the next month, your brain will focus not only on noticing characteristics you hadn't noticed before, but also on finding common characteristics.

The brain is so powerful that it will always find common characteristics. Indeed, it often takes only three points of support to justify any proposition – and you will be able to find at least three common characteristics.

Answer: car crash mind-opening practice

Sometimes people think of a stepfather/stepson relationship. Sometimes they suggest that the boy's father got out of the wreck quickly, went by helicopter and so beat the boy to the hospital. Sometimes there are answers that involve the clerical use of the phrase 'my son' and the assumption that the doctor was also a padre or a priest.

But it's only a very limited mindset that stops you thinking of the solution that the doctor was the boy's mother.

Shame on you, and in these emancipated times too!

The picture in your mind of a doctor being a man restricts your ability to solve the problem, which is otherwise very easy.

What can we learn?

What we can learn from the car crash and pet owners mind-opening practices illustrates two points about mindsets.

First, it is very easy to have a limiting mindset. In the car crash mind opener, this is also an unarticulated mindset, a blockage you hardly realize is there. If you were asked 'Are all doctors men?' or even 'Is a doctor usually a man?' you would probably answer in the negative. Your limitation is not an overt one, it is hidden. Of course, once you have experienced an exercise like this, you rarely get caught on this particular limitation again.

But if you have such an unarticulated limiting mindset on this simple logical problem, imagine how many you have on business problems. Imagine the number of occasions that people in your organization are operating to limiting mindsets without realizing it.

There will be hidden assumptions about a particular department's attitude, such that your mind is sensitive to any data that supports your assumption and reinforces it – probably in an inaccurate or unproductive way. There will be similar unarticulated mindsets about certain individuals, perhaps customers, even limiting hidden assumptions about female managers on the part of male managers and vice versa.

Secondly, it is easy to find data to support an overt limiting mindset and to focus only on this data, not seeing data which would support the opposite. In the pet owners mind opener, people focus only on the two or three points of similarity which support the mindset and on this basis it becomes 'true'; they ignore the thousand or more points that are counter to this and would render it untrue.

How many times are you and your organization doing this day by day?

Now that we have more and more information to select from, the opportunity for falling into this trap becomes significantly bigger. For example, in a global company with operations in perhaps up to 100 countries, it will probably always be possible to find data from three or four countries to count as examples to prove any mindset you choose.

The third point about mindsets is that it is very easy to pick up a limiting mindset and follow it down a dead end. The mechanism is as follows.

THE SILK EXERCISE

Focus on the word silk:

SILK SILK SILK SILK SILK SILK SILK SILK SILK SILK
SILK SILK SILK SILK SILK SILK SILK SILK SILK SILK
SILK SILK SILK SILK SILK SILK SILK SILK SILK SILK
SILK SILK SILK SILK SILK SILK SILK SILK SILK SILK
SILK SILK SILK SILK SILK SILK SILK SILK SILK SILK
SILK SILK SILK SILK SILK SILK SILK SILK SILK SILK

Now say the word 'silk' out loud 12 times. As you say 'silk', count out the number of times by putting up one finger, then another and so on, up to 12.

Say it six times, louder, counting each out on your fingers.
Then say it three times, really loud. Do it.
Now, what do cows drink?

THE SILK EXERCISE: DISCUSSION

What do cows drink? Cows don't drink milk: they drink water.

Three things often happen in this exercise.

First, individuals operate according to a very limiting mindset. They tell their brain something along the following lines: 'I'm about to be tricked into saying 'silk' when I shouldn't. Don't let me be a fool and say 'silk' when I shouldn't.' When cows come up, the association is milk and the brain accepts this as a solution to the mindset of 'whatever you do, avoid silk'.

The second thing that happens, in groups, is that you realize that other people are answering 'milk' so you don't question your own answer. 'The rest of the organization is thinking like this, so it must be right.' Even if the question is repeated, you will stick to the answer 'milk' because everyone else is saying it.

Finally, there will be some individuals who, having committed themselves to the answer 'milk', will adopt a defensive mindset and continue to think they are right and that there must be, somewhere, a cow that does drink milk. There isn't – although, of course, calves do drink milk from their mothers. And some people and organizations will want to adopt an attitude of trying to show they were right, even though they weren't. And they will do this to justify a mindset that is unimportant and was picked up in a nano-second. They do this in order to keep their pride. The mindset of defending personal pride is a very limiting one and is dealt with specifically later.

Adopt powerful not limiting mindsets

In the early 1980s, I became general manager of P&G's Greek subsidiary, in the Middle East division, different to the rest of western Europe. We were due to launch Always, a sanitary napkin brand, along with western Europe. This was simultaneously being test marketed in the South of France. Western Europe decided not to go ahead at that stage. It subsequently did so, some five years later, with great results.

The issue the Greek subsidiary was faced with was whether to postpone, as western Europe had, or to try to go ahead on its own.

It would have been easy to adopt a limiting mindset, in line with the overall company mood of not being ready. There were many issues regarding the brand on which one could adopt a limiting mindset and find all the reasons to postpone.

But, in fact, because of the business situation in Greece, we were almost forced to adopt a powerful mindset to help make the project work.

The Greek subsidiary had historically relied heavily on a large detergent business. But the outlook for this was not good: it was subject to severe government price controls and restrictive government procedures for introducing new products. The only option for the Greek subsidiary was to diversify. We had to adopt a positive mindset about making projects like Always work, because we couldn't build a profitable subsidiary from our detergent base.

The mindsets which would lead to the project not working were all reasonable. For example:

➤ The product category couldn't be advertised on Greek television, for reasons of taste.

➤ The Always product couldn't be significantly premium priced versus local competitive brands, particularly in view of the low per capita income in Greece.

➤ It would be difficult to get Greek women to change from their traditional habits and brands – they would stay with current practices rather than trying something new.

➤ The new Always top sheet would be rejected by traditional Greek women and they wouldn't try it.

➤ The Greek subsidiary couldn't go it alone on the brand without the support of simultaneous work going on in other western European countries.

Once such limiting mindsets were adopted, there would have been plenty of data to select to support them and to postpone the project.

Instead, for each limiting mindset a more powerful one was adopted and different, more enabling action steps were identified:

➤ If we could break through the problem of the ban on sanitary napkin advertising, advertising the product advantages of Always would make a huge impact on the Greek consumer. The brand group did get the TV authorities to agree to Always advertising, first by agreeing to advertise after 9 pm, then by getting agreement to superior absorbency demonstrations without the physical pad being shown, and finally getting agreement to advertising without these constraints.

➤ If we could find a way to make premium pricing versus local competitors acceptable, the project would be profitable and viable. The brand group did manage to make premium pricing acceptable. After all, the actual usage of sanitary napkins is relatively low – they are only used for one week a month. The actual premium cost of using Always for those occasions, versus a competitive brand, was less than the price of a cup of coffee a month. And the better absorbency and protection of Always more than made that worthwhile for the Greek consumer.

➤ If we could find a way to get Greek women to experience the superior performance of Always, they would be prepared to change from their current products. The brand group found effective ways to sample the new Always product – going door to door and giving the correct size samples for each woman in the household, making Always a product they would jointly consider and try.

➤ If we could find a way to help traditional consumers consider the feel of the top sheet in an acceptable way, they would appreciate its superior performance. The brand group invented a new term for the top sheet, Alveonet, which helped bring connotations of the dry feeling the consumer experienced with it.

➤ If we could find a way to attract staff group and expert resource from other countries to help Greece, it wouldn't matter that western Europe was postponing. The brand group found that visiting Greece could be made one of the more enjoyable business experiences for any staff group or helpful expert.

In the end, by adopting powerful mindsets instead of accepting limiting ones, the Always project was made to work for Greece. The brand was launched nationally and became one of the biggest successes of Always in any country, anywhere in the world.

Double the profit – why it can't be done

It is very easy to adopt limiting mindsets and then find all the data that supports and justifies them. This particularly happens when we are challenged to do something we previously haven't achieved. To accept a mindset that it might be possible almost implies that previous performance has been unsatisfactory. To accept the challenge could somehow get misinterpreted that previously we weren't trying.

Therefore a frequent organizational response is to say 'It can't be done' and to assemble all the reasons why not. Thus it becomes a self-fulfilling prophecy that it can't be achieved.

Consider an organization that has been reasonably profitable and growing steadily, with profit growth of 5–10 percent a year. It is challenged to step-change the profitability of the operation within a short time, say to double it within two years.

The frequent reaction to such a challenge is to reject it on the basis that it simply can't be done – or it would have been done already.

The organization will explain all the reasons that have prevented, and will prevent, that breakthrough level of profit being achieved:

➤ We can't reduce the cost of the products, because that will reduce quality and we'll lose sales. This mindset will be supported by selected previous instances of failure trying this approach.

➤ We can't increase the price because that will lose sales, volume and more profit than we gain. Examples of this happening will be identified in support.

➤ We can't reduce the marketing expense because that will lose us sales and more profit than we gain. Examples of this approach will be quoted in support of the fact it can't be done.

➤ On the other hand, if we increase marketing support, that will cost more money but won't necessarily move short-term sales because the market is stagnant, so profit will go down because of the extra cost. Examples from history, or from other businesses, will be quoted to show why this approach won't work either.

➤ We can't reduce the cost of our salesforce because that will mean fewer people, fewer calls on customers, fewer sales and so less profit. Examples of the failure of this approach will be quoted.

➤ We can't reduce our overhead cost because that will reduce the number of projects we can do and put at risk the sort of things that have brought us our current success. A full list will be produced of all the important things that couldn't be done if we reduced overhead cost.

So according to these mindsets it can't be done: profit can't be doubled in two years.

It's important to realize that there is no dishonesty involved here. No one is lying. No one is deliberately being obstructive or awkward. No one is exaggerating or misinterpreting history deliberately.

It is just that once you adopt a limiting mindset, your brain focuses on searching for arguments, facts and examples that support it.

And your brain, honestly and genuinely, misses the data that would not be supportive – because it's not looking for it. We'll return to this example later.

MIND-OPENING PRACTICE: TELLING THE TIME

How good a judge of time are you? Without looking at your watch, guess what the time is, right now. Say out loud what your guess is. Now check.

You may be quite accurate.

Now, without looking at your watch again, answer the question: 'What does the number six on your watch face look like?' Is it a regular one, a Roman numeral, a dash, a dot, a double dash – what? Don't look at your watch but make a decision and say it out loud.

This shouldn't be a very difficult task. After all, you've just looked at your watch. Now check and see for yourself.

It is quite surprising how many people get the answer wrong.

People may have looked at their watch 20,000 times already – but they won't know what the number six looks like.

Ah, people say, when I look at my watch I don't look at it to see what the number six looks like, I look at it to tell the time.

And that's exactly the point. It depends on your mindset. If you look at your watch with the normal mindset, you don't even see the six. If you were to look at your watch with the mindset of admiring the pattern, the clock face, the figures, of course you'd notice.

Mind on the lookout

The learning from the telling-the-time mind opener is important. There is so much information and data and signals around us that the brain has to be selective about what gets processed, about what it decides to notice rather than just see. How many times do we see things without noticing them, probably because they aren't relevant to what we're thinking about? How many times do we hear things without listening to them – because we just can't listen to everything our ears hear?

Imagine the number of things your eyes see each minute of the day, the number of things your ears hear each minute, the number of body language signals, the number of things in the background. Consider all the signals emitting from all the people you see each day, all the things you see at home, at work, traveling to work and back. Your brain has to choose which to notice and consider or it will be overloaded. We necessarily make ourselves oblivious to most of it. It goes in one eye and out the other, in one ear and out the other.

Beyond what the brain has to choose to focus on from current input, it also contains a vast universe of experiences and data – a gigantic memory bank. All sorts of memories and instances and experiences can be triggered by something you see or hear. 'That reminds me' or 'something comes to mind' are common phrases to describe this. In fact, most of the things coming into your mind are triggered out of memory.

What the brain selects to focus on from all this is determined by the mindsets we choose – by the way we set our minds.

So choosing a mindset that 'something will be impossible to achieve' directs the brain to select, from current input and memory, all the facts and arguments and examples that support it.

Choosing a mindset that 'it should be possible' directs the brain to select, from current input and memory, all the bits and pieces that might be relevant to achieving it.

If you want to achieve breakthrough results, the second mindset is more powerful.

This is the basis on which positive thinking and specific goal setting work. Once you firmly commit to a specific goal, your brain is set to seek out and spot anything that helps. That's why people say that once you fully commit to a goal, 'things just happen' to help it. It's not a miracle. The mind has been set to pick up things and opportunities that will help towards the breakthrough goal.

For example, assume you were running a business and were reconsidering what medium to use for your advertising. Up to now you haven't used outdoor advertising, i.e. posters and hoardings. You have just used newspaper and magazine advertising. But you are now actively considering whether outdoor advertising would be effective and in particular what sort of posters or hoardings would work.

Suddenly, your brain notices all sorts of posters and hoardings on the way to work, from the car, from the train window and walking down the street. You might have traveled this route hundreds of times and not noticed these before, until you became interested in outdoor advertising.

What all this amounts to is putting the brain on the lookout for particular types of data or opportunity. The mindsets you adopt are the ways you are asking the brain to be on the lookout. The brain cannot absorb or register every single signal it receives – it has to be selective. It's your choice what it selects and what it doesn't.

I'll believe it when I see it
or
I'll see it when I believe it?

Limiting mindsets are a poor choice – just like negative thoughts. They focus the brain on spotting data and memories that reinforce the limitation.

Powerful mindsets focus the brain on spotting data and memories that help you achieve breakthrough results.

Consider some typical business mindsets that can develop between the local operation on the ground and the distant headquarters. The local operation often feels that it receives instructions or guidelines that make no sense in the local market. Some seem impractical and out of touch with what's happening at the coalface.

At the same time, some of the actions the local operation takes seem strange to headquarters. Sometimes a local operation may seem to be repeating a mistake and not using experience that has been expensively brought elsewhere. Or they may be taking an action that looks positive for them but has bigger, negative effects elsewhere.

Over time two mindsets can be developed:

➤ In the local operation: headquarters don't know the local realities
➤ In headquarters: the local operation can't see the big picture.

Once both parts of the operation start thinking this way, they'll find more and more instances to support these attitudes.

The first-line people can find more and more instances of headquarters being out of touch with the reality of what's happening at the coalface. Headquarters, meanwhile, can find all sorts of instances of the local operation not doing the best thing because they can't see the whole picture.

Once these mindsets are solidified, it becomes very difficult for the two parts of the organization to work well together. Every suggestion from headquarters is dismissed as being of low value by the local operation. Every input or suggestion from the local operation is discounted by headquarters.

The alternative, more powerful mindset, for both parts of the operation, is for each to look both at the wood and the trees – and to do this together.

The ultimate limiting mindset: 'it can't be done'

This is probably the most damaging limiting mindset. It focuses the energies of people and organizations on finding why things won't work, why goals are too tough and impossible to achieve and all the barriers and problems. Logic and persuasion are used to assemble all these in a way that supports the position that it can't be done. And then it can't be.

We're all aware of such attitudes. Examples are:

➤ 'We've tried it in the past, and it won't work.' As a result, it doesn't get tried again, even though circumstances have changed or it may not be exactly what was tried in the past. Moreover, most things that are worthwhile don't work first time and need perseverance and adjustment that they may not have received last time around.

➤ 'We know our answer is right.' And so no other answer is possible or appropriate – let alone better. As a result, no new approach gets considered, even though it may give significantly better results.

➤ 'Based on the facts, it won't work.' And so again it doesn't get tried with full commitment. But these facts may not be complete or even real and other people's experiences may be different, indeed even more pertinent.

➤ 'There's nothing in that idea.' And so it doesn't get considered. It gets dismissed out of hand, even if the idea would in reality bring discontinuous results.

➤ 'From my point of view, it won't work.' But is this really the only way to look at it, the only possible point of view?

➤ 'There's no way that can work.' There won't be a way it will work unless you find one.

➤ 'I know I'm right, it won't work.' In this situation, if it depends on your input or commitment to work, then you're right that it won't work. You need to adopt the mindset: 'How can I make it work?'

These limiting mindsets are so common that it is worth developing common and systematic approaches to change them into more powerful mindsets.

Chapter 9 introduces the concept of Mindsoftware. These are valuable pieces of software for your cranial computer, in much the same way as you seek useful software for your personal computer.

At the back of this book there are details of Mindsoftware to help change these very common limiting mindsets into more powerful ones. These are designed to be used at any time – in a meeting or on your own; or sent to someone else in the organization to help position a point; or sent on fax cover sheets.

Their key advantage is that they can turn these very common, 'can't be done', limiting mindsets into more powerful ones which will help achieve step-change results.

MIND-OPENING PRACTICE: ON THE LOOKOUT

If you need more convincing, try this exercise, on your own or in a group.

Ask people to look around the room and notice everything in it that is blue. Look at the walls, the ceiling, the floor, behind you, close up, far away, everywhere. Spend a minute or two doing it now.

Now ask people to close their eyes, rest their head on their arms and remember the room they've just looked at. They should then call out everything they can remember that was green.

Having focused on blue, they'll be able to recollect very little green.

Ask them to open their eyes and look around at everything that is green that they missed.

The lesson is that a limited mindset puts the mind on the lookout selectively for the data that supports it.

A fixed mindset

The previous examples should illustrate how easy it is to adopt a fixed mindset and then to focus selectively on information that supports it.

> The eye sees in this what it looks for and it looks for what is already in the mind
> Motto of the Scientific School of Police in Paris

This is the reason that so many people find they can believe in their horoscopes: a horoscope suggests that something will be true that is broad enough for you subsequently to be able to identify one or two instances, examples or events that seem to confirm it.

This is also the reason placebos work. The patient adopts the mindset that they will get better and then identifies those symptoms that support it.

However, it becomes incredibly limiting if the mindset you or the organization adopts is a limiting one and if it stays fixed for a long time. Remember the saying:

Frederick the Great (1712–86) lost the Battle of Jena (1806)

The mindset of a fixed way of warfare lasted long after Frederick's death and was unable to cope with dramatically changed conditions 20 years later.

This is why kings used to have a fool or court jester. The role these people played was to adopt contrary or silly ways of looking at things to help prevent the king getting into a fixed, limiting mindset. Remember, many a true word is spoken in jest.

There is a choice

The fact that there is a choice is the secret of this strategy. We can choose which mindsets to follow and adopt. Take, for example, people who have favorite mottos or proverbs by which they live. They will point out example after example from everyday life of instances which support that their proverb or motto is right. 'See, I told you so; better safe than sorry; there you are, another example.'

But often there is a completely opposite proverb that is also true, on other occasions. There is evidence from life, from folklore, to support each of the opposites. You can simply choose which one you want to adopt, in which situations, as you go about life.

Of course, it is also easy to choose a proverb for an organization – and the action steps it takes, and the results it achieves, will depend on the proverb or mindset it adopts.

ONE MINDSET	ANOTHER MINDSET
Better safe than sorry	Nothing ventured, nothing gained
Absence makes the heart grow fonder	Out of sight, out of mind
Many hands make light work	Too many cooks spoil the broth
You can't teach an old dog new tricks	It's never too late to learn

The organization that adopts the mindset 'You can't teach an old dog new tricks' will do different things when training its people, and get different results, from one that chooses 'It's never too late to learn'.

The organization that chooses the mindset 'Nothing ventured, nothing gained' will generate different action to the organization that adopts 'Better safe than sorry'.

To achieve breakthrough results, it's best to choose to avoid mindsets that limit you – and choose to have your brain work on powerful mindsets.

Changing your mindset is a form of creative *and* logical thinking. It's exactly the sort of approach that brings the new, productive thinking you are looking for.

From limiting to powerful mindsets

Industry-transforming mindsets

Running/track shoes

Recall what happened to the running shoe/track shoe business when someone chose a new mindset: 'We're not in the business of supplying athletics shoes to athletes; we're in the business of supplying leisure shoes to everyone. Everyone should wear our trainers as leisure shoes.'

Pens

Recall what happened to the pen business when someone chose a new mindset: 'We're not in the business of supplying pens to people who need a new one; we're in the business of providing gifts for people to give their loved ones!' That change in mindset changed actions and approaches to packaging, pricing and marketing.

Watches

And recall what happened to the watch industry when someone chose a new mindset: 'We're not in the business of selling timepieces; we're in the business of selling fashion accessories.' This change of mindset transformed the fortunes of Swatch and the Swiss watch industry.

There have been many such changes in mindsets that have transformed businesses:

➤ Restaurants traditionally tried to gain a competitive edge through the calibre of their staff – excellent chefs and excellent service. McDonald's started by adopting the mindset of minimizing staff to cope with the shortage of labor during the Second World War.

➤ Cars used to be built by bringing in different teams of workers to a static position where a car was being built. Ford changed all this after visiting a meat-packing line. It adopted the mindset of bringing the work to the workers and so invented the assembly line.

➤ Retail shops traditionally brought goods to the customer. The first supermarket decided to bring the customer to the goods.

➤ Television news programs used to have the mindset that news had to be transmitted in relatively short, edited bursts at fixed times in the evening. The mindset was to compete only via the caliber and personality of the newscasters. CNN adopted a different mindset – that people would be interested in news as it breaks, whatever time of day.

➤ Banks always had the mindset that all customers wanted personal attention. Hole-in-the-wall cash machines challenged this and made the opposite mindset work.

Often an organization changes its mindsets as a result of a change of people. Is it that the new person is necessarily that much more innately able than their predecessor? Often not. It's just that they bring a fresh approach.

Imagine the power that an organization will achieve if it finds ways to choose a more powerful mindset without having to change people.

The power of an organization is more related to its ability to choose new mindsets than it is to the cumulative IQs of the people within it

Consider, as a contrast, our previous double-the-profit example and the sort of good thinking that could be inspired, given a more powerful mindset.

Double the profit – new mindsets

Choose a mindset that it might be possible to double profits in two years and consider how it might be done if you had to do it.

➤ With this more powerful mindset, the organization may find that products are overengineered and that a change in product – to one of lower cost – might well not be noticeable or important to customers. Indeed, by eliminating cost in some aspects of the product that are of low importance, it might be possible to fund an improvement in an aspect of higher importance, while still reducing cost overall. And if this concept wasn't applicable to all products, the powerful mindset might help you find that it was applicable to some.

➤ With this more powerful mindset, the organization may find that products are not as price sensitive as was thought and that price increases can be taken. And if this wasn't applicable to all the products, it might be found to be applicable to some products or some sizes or even some variants — at least some of the time.

➤ With this more powerful mindset, the organization may find that not all the marketing expense is very effective at driving sales. You could identify the least effective 20 percent and take half of that to improve profit, investing the other half to reinforce those marketing activities which are driving sales.

➤ With this more powerful mindset, the organization may find that by eliminating all the sales calls that bring only very small returns for the effort, and refocusing some of that time on more calls to higher potential customers, both the costs of the salesforce could go down and the volume of sales go up. This improves profit in two ways.

➤ With this more powerful mindset, the organization may find that sales of some products are not profitable. By eliminating them, profits go up. Similarly, some variants may be far less profitable than others. By eliminating these, customers may switch to the other variants which are far more profitable.

➤ With this more powerful mindset, the organization may find that by reducing overhead costs and concentrating only on the most important projects, profits may be increased.

Most positive self-talk is a way of helping you adopt a powerful mindset, as opposed to getting trapped in a negative one. When this is done in a whole-brained way, it releases power and passion that generate positive action.

Consider the following mottoes to help drive you and the organization towards breakthrough results:

➤ Some people walk in the rain, others just get wet
➤ The man on the top of the mountain didn't fall there
➤ Some people dream of worthy accomplishments, while others lay awake and do them
➤ Accept the challenges, so you may feel the exhilaration of victory
➤ No one can predict to what height you can soar: even you will not know until you spread your wings.

The Seventh
Thinking Strategy

Hats, maps and thinking pads

versus

Meetings and memos

9 *Hats, Maps and Thinking Pads*

In the 1950s, psychologists estimated that the average person used 50% of brain capacity. In the 1960s and 1970s, the estimate was lowered to 10%. In the 1990s the best guess is 0.01% or less.

Michael J Gelb, High Performance Learning

You won't get breakthrough results by continuing all your current habits and practices in the same way as before. But at the same time you and the organization probably feel it's difficult to change your routines and procedures. Indeed, many people feel that the whole culture has to change.

Don't try to change the culture, just change the habits. If you change habits on only two activities – meetings and memos – you will make an enormous difference. Meetings and memos of one sort or another absorb 80 percent of an organization's time and talent.

Tackling and reinventing the habits and practices of meetings and memos is the simplest and easiest way to use your talent and time more effectively for breakthrough results. And it doesn't have to be every meeting, every memo. Start with one, spread to another.

Moreover, anyone who has the power to call a meeting or write a memo has the power to change the norm for meetings or memos. Anyone who attends as a participant has the power and opportunity – and, we could say, the duty – to suggest change.

Later in this chapter we'll look at new tools – hats, maps and thinking pads – to spend your time on, on your own or with others, to take the place of your traditional activities in meetings and memos. And you'll find ways to get intensely interested and attracted to these tools. They are stimulating, fun and enormously effective at helping towards breakthrough results.

But, as with all the strategies, it's not enough to get attracted and interested in the juicy carrot. It's as important to use the crippling stick of intense dissatisfaction with the current waste of talent and time in meetings and memos.

How many of the last decade's bestselling business books talk about meetings and memos as crucial to breakthrough performance? Very few. How often does the subject receive serious attention from business leaders, management gurus or business school academics? Very seldom. Most of the time this subject is treated as a skill to be delegated to the training department or to be learnt on training courses. Yet some of the bestselling business books of recent years have been about a cartoon character called Dilbert. He pokes fun at our ridiculous behavior in meetings, memos and conversations. These books outsell many books by the best-known guru or the most-respected business school professor on reengineering, quality, business transformation, the digital world and the like.

And why? For three reasons. First, the stupid behavior they illustrate is a real reflection of the triviality going on in most meetings and memos. Second, a huge number of people are caught up wasting their time and energy in such trivialities. And it's these people who buy Dilbert books to have the opportunity to laugh at the banal stupidities they encounter every day. If this wasn't so serious, it would be funny.

The third reason is also simple. Dilbert books treat the issue in a whole-brained way. They use pictures, humor and emotion. That's very different from the boring, left-brained-only, no-pictures business book you have to 'study'.

Imagine the total amount of talent and time that is caught up in such banalities every day. And imagine the contribution if we could release that talent and time to work towards breakthrough results.

The rate of change and non-change

Consider the phenomenal rate of change going on both in society and in the business world. Not only is the current decade very different to the last; the last five years are very different to the previous five and even next year will be very different to this year.

Within this, phenomenal technological changes have also taken place in the area of business communications that weren't available a few years ago. And these are the changes that have already happened, let alone the technologies to come.

In recent years, we've had:

➤ telephone conference calls between different people in different locations
➤ mobile phones
➤ voice mail
➤ sophisticated answering machines with remote access
➤ videotape messages
➤ remote transmission of dictation
➤ videoconferencing
➤ PC videoconferencing
➤ satellite links for presentations and seminars
➤ e-mail
➤ mobile faxes
➤ the Internet.

More and more people are using the very latest hardware and software. Moreover, the rate of change in their capability is quite astronomical.

It's now better and easier to get a new model PC than to try to upgrade an 'old' one, which may itself be no more than a year or so old.

Against this background, consider the following mind opener.

MIND-OPENING PRACTICE: FOLD YOUR ARMS

This is very simple. Fold your arms. Go on, do it now. Put down the book and fold your arms. Take the risk!

Now, how did you decide whether to put your left arm over your right or your right over your left? You didn't. You just did it out of habit.

Here is a proposition for you. Despite the rate of change, you have given no more quality of thought to how you operate in meetings and memos than you do to how you fold your arms. You simply repeat old habits, unquestioningly.

You are probably operating with the same habits and practices this year as you did last – in fact, the same as you did five or ten years ago. Some people have the same habits and practices that they used over 20 years ago!

The world has changed enormously since then. There is 'software' available to get more out of your mind and talent, just as there is new hardware and technology. Get with it!

Meetings and memos: non-change

Despite the availability of new alternatives to meetings, how many are the same as they've always been and just as unproductive? In fact, many organizations respond to a complex world by having more meetings rather than fewer.

How many are still held in the same time, same place, like some form of unthinking historical ritual? Indeed, how many of the participants even sit in the same seats, the same places?

And how many meetings are there? Do you know how many meetings take place in your organization? Count them. How many people-hours are involved each week?

How many meetings do you attend each week? What percentage of your own time is involved this way? If you don't know, work it out. You may well be surprised.

And how many memos do you still receive each day, hard copy or electronic? Count them! And how many of them really help you achieve step-change, breakthrough results? How many of them are written in a style that stimulates or inspires you to greater things?

Junk activities at work

We eat junk food. We describe many TV programs as junk. A lot of what comes through our letterboxes is junk mail. Junk is all around us.

We need to expand the junk concept to work activities. Few people do anything about junk mail at work. In fact, in many organizations the arrival of e-mail has spawned even more junk mail than existed before. We have junk e-mail, junk memos, junk copies, junk comments, junk meetings, junk questions, junk presentations.

Imagine how much more effective you and your organization would be if you identified and eliminated junk activities.

At the same time, how much time do you really have to think? How much time do you have to create new ways, to design a better, different future?

Similarly, what activities do you, or others, do to help you adopt a fresh mind, a new outlook? To adopt an open mind, instead of persisting with closed attitudes almost without realizing it?

Are you so caught up with junk activities that you have no time for creative thought?

The issue, of course, is that it's not easy to get rid of junk activities. It's not enough to identify them – although this sort of decision helps and is a minor push back that might temper their escalation.

The only way forward is to generate alternative, quality activities. And little by little these activities assume priority and so displace the junk – or consign it to the figurative junk basket. Just like eating well: you eat something else that means junk food no longer has a place.

This is replacing the bricks and mortar, piece by piece. Here we'll discuss how to do it for the two biggest areas of junk activity: meetings and memos.

Meetings

You can make things better by incrementalism: fewer meetings, fewer attendees, more focused, shorter and so on.

Technology helps. For example, the advent of the videoconference did improve matters. The meeting tends to start and finish on time because the line or facility has been booked for a limited time. Also only one person speaks at a time because otherwise the video call doesn't work. Similarly, people listen a little better – the time delay forces this. And, moreover, people ration their personal airtime more – it's more obvious when one person hogs all the talking.

But this is nothing more than incrementalism. Most meetings still underuse the talent and tacit knowledge of the people attending them. Indeed, many meetings end up with poorer action steps than any single individual could have come up with on their own. What can be done?

Meetings everywhere, in every organization, display several diseases. These are contagious and spread from meeting to meeting, thus helping form the culture of the organization.

Eight meeting diseases

1 The verbal IQ trap
2 Groupthink disease
3 Idea destruction disease

4 More bias disease

5 A vs B disease

6 Collaboration disease

7 Fear of exposure disease

8 Politics disease

The verbal IQ trap

The symptoms of this disease are that the decision or position coming out of a meeting has been overly influenced by the verbal dexterity of one or two participants. These people are in the trap of a high verbal IQ. Because they are able to express two or three arguments in favor of a point of view, they become convinced that this is the best point of view and continue to advocate it. Moreover, if they can, on the spur of the moment, deal with other people's spontaneous objections, their point of view becomes more and more entrenched.

For global companies, this trap is even bigger. The point of view of those with a better command of English (or whatever is the dominant language) can hold sway over those whose native language is different.

Yet the point of view or position adopted could be completely wrong for the business situation. It may be a far poorer solution than many others, if only time were taken to think, generate and consider alternatives.

Looked at objectively, it's a real error to allow decision making in a forum that can be so afflicted by the verbal IQ disease as to lead to sub-optimum results. It is incrementalism rather than triΔngular thinking.

Groupthink disease

The symptoms of groupthink normally occur about two-thirds of the way through any meeting. Realizing that time is passing, the group starts to coalesce around a particular viewpoint or position. A 'group thought' starts to emerge.

Beyond that point, any different or counter thought is considered unhelpful. So even if the best idea or thought emerges after this, it may not even be voiced, for fear of the contributor being considered counter-productive, dragging things out, making the meeting go on too long and so on.

Idea destruction disease

This disease involves the verbal destruction of any idea that is not fully developed and doesn't have fully established defences.

If an idea proposed in a meeting is 80 percent right but 20 percent plain wrong, what happens? With glee – and sometimes with malice – one or more participants will focus on the 20 percent that is wrong. So much can be said about how wrong the 20 percent is that the proposer is described as talking nonsense. And with this comes the automatic assumption that the other 80 percent is also wrong.

Quite soon people learn that it's too risky to propose an idea. Moreover, even if an idea gets accepted and later proves not to work out in practice, the originator is forever associated with an idea that didn't work. And the more spectacularly it fails, the more stupid the originator is considered to be.

Instead of acting as a devil's advocate in a meeting, pointing out what is wrong with an idea, why not be an angel's advocate, making it clear what is right? Treat ideas like seeds – put them into flowerpots and then into a greenhouse to allow them to grow and get stronger, before being subjected to the rigors of the outdoor garden.

Or treat a 'failed' idea as a 'miss' instead of a 'mistake'. Sometimes you need to miss once or twice to correct your aim.

More bias disease

The symptoms of this disease are a tendency for the same group, meeting regularly, to become more and more biased in the direction of the majority. So if the majority are conservative, and only a few are prepared to take risks, over time the whole group becomes more and more conservative, leading to more and more incrementalism.

The opposite is often mistakenly thought to happen: a group will settle down to the average level of the participants. What happens in practice is that group norms start to filter out the comments of the minority. The minority feel that their comments are unappreciated and stop making them. Those in the majority get more and more confidence that their bias is appropriate and make more and more remarks that feed off one another.

Thus, for example, a group of people who are individually only mildly left-wing in attitude will over time become more left-wing than any one individual within it.

Put differently, without an intervention, a group with a limited mindset, meeting regularly without cross-fertilization, will become more and more ingrained in that limited mindset as a result of the meetings.

A vs B disease

The symptoms of this are polarity and argument around two different options, when creation of a third or fourth option may well be the best solution. Here verbal dexterity in support of one, or criticizing the other, absorbs all the talent and time. Individuals seek examples and instances to support A vs B.

Often whoever is fastest on their feet with the best information, or examples in support, 'wins' for A vs B – even if more considered thought would produce the opposite and conclude that B is better and even in a situation where an undeveloped C or D would be better still.

Collaboration disease

One symptom of collaboration disease is a desire to be seen to get on well with the rest of the team, to be a good team player. The result is that people don't introduce fresh facts and alternative points of view often enough.

Moreover, once they've given an alternative point of view once or twice, they refrain from doing it a third time – even if the third time is the most important – for fear of being typecast as awkward.

Fear of exposure disease

The symptoms of this disease include clear concern about risking expressing ignorance by asking 'Why?' in a meeting. By the same token, there can be fear of exposure that expresses itself as reluctance to admit that other ideas are better than our own. The result is that attempts to explore ideas further are rejected.

Politics disease

When meetings suffer from this disease politics becomes the acceptable norm. What is said in a meeting is heavily influenced by personal and departmental positioning. This also influences what is *not* said. It influences when things are said in the meeting, by whom, to whom, against whom. This constrains the ability of the meeting to utilize fully the talent and knowledge of the participants.

How does all this make you feel? Do you yet feel hugely dissatisfied with standard meetings as the way to get the best out of your time and talent? Don't you feel ashamed that meetings you have been in have displayed one and probably more of the above diseases? Is this really the way you want to spend your life and life time?

Memos

The second likely source of junk activity is memos. Some, a few, are great, but time spent on memos in general is a huge absorption of talent and brains – for relatively little result. These are far better ways in which talent and brains can be deployed.

Junk memos are increasing despite all our other means of communication. In the UK in 1980, 20.1 billion sheets of A4 paper were used. In 1995, the figure was 103.5 billion: mind-boggling.

Organizational cancer

Consider what happens to a single memo and the way it clogs up the organization's talent. There are at least nine ways in which a memo absorbs the talent and time.

1 Memo-compositis
2 Address-too-many-itis
3 Copy-the-boss-itis
4 Copy-subordinate-itis
5 Copy-peers-itis
6 Study-memos-itis
7 Copy-on-itis
8 For-the-record-itis
9 Responditis

Memo-compositis

Composing a memo takes time and effort that could often be better spent on other things. You can't think creatively when you're writing. Your mind is clogged up with thinking about the structure, the order, the wording and the support for what you want to say.

And whatever you want to say, you'll be able to find some information, somewhere, to support it. There is so much information pollution it's easy to find some to support a point of view or a suggestion.

But the act of composing a memo is merely the tip of the iceberg of its effects through the organization.

Address-too-many-itis

This is a common cause of the spread of the disease. Writing to several people at once is often unproductive. They all feel the need to reply, they often copy each other and you end up with a dog's breakfast.

Copy-the-boss-itis

This causes further stresses and strains and posturing. It increases the amount of wheel spinning, your memo going to and fro.

Copy-subordinate-itis

The same as above but in reverse – just as bad.

Copy-peers-itis

Again, you end up with a dog's breakfast. Copying too many people to avoid 'why-wasn't-I-copied-itis'.

Study-memos-itis

You think that memos have to be studied – not read. It's very hard work. It's left-brained-only graft. The more there are, the tougher it is, like a long slog of homework. And all this activity dulls the mind.

Copy-on-itis

Often it's unclear from the list of addressees and those copied whether the memo is meant to have a circulation that is as few as possible or alternatively all those likely to be affected. Most fall in between. The recipient assumes therefore that the strategy is all those likely to be affected and can think of several people in this category who haven't already been copied, so copies the memo on to them.

For-the-record-itis

This causes even greater likelihood of further memos in response. Even if a memo is only indirectly critical of their operation or function, or even if only incidentally to do with their patch, people feel that a response is required. Otherwise the 5 or 15 percent that is incorrect from your viewpoint will be deemed to be correct for ever after – because it's in writing.

For many people there's an assumption that whatever is in writing is correct. This is a different convention to discussion, where often you will let points pass, even if you disagree, because they're not absolutely crucial to the issue. You can't spend your time correcting every point of view or statement you don't agree with. But in writing, things assume a bigger importance. They're on file.

Responditis

The recipients engage in memo–compositis and start the above process again. And this happens for each and every recipient.

Going round in circles

These memo diseases form circles of activity that are repeated until the issue stops. Extra secondary circles are formed by each recipient of the original memo – talk about going round in circles.

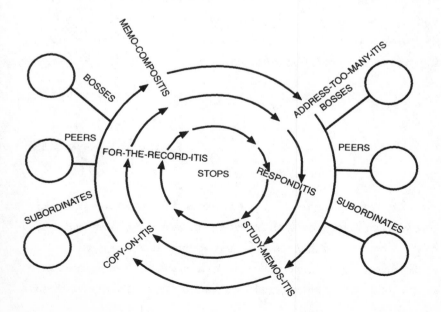

All the above applies equally to e-mail, if not more so, leading to ever-increasing information pollution and ever-increasing clogging up of the organization's arteries.

Getting hugely dissatisfied with meetings and memos

Hasn't this chapter made you feel hugely dissatisfied with wasting your life away on meetings and memos? Do you really want to be such a bureaucrat, going through life in neutral? Aren't you ashamed that you participate in such petty and inconsequential activities and have never sought to change them?

Possibly by now you are so embarrassed you are becoming defensive. After all, this is how you spend much of your time and talent so it must be useful. And you can think of many examples where meetings and memos are useful.

But remember the 'pet owners look like their pets' syndrome. Out of defensiveness, you are looking for good examples to support why your current activity is worthwhile. Now do the opposite. For the next few weeks look for examples of the waste of talent and time in meetings and memos. You'll be horrified.

Three new tools

How can you replace your current activities? There are three new tools that you can engage on with others, or on your own, to replace some of the activities and diseases currently sapping your energies.

Before doing so, however, let's consider the VCR syndrome. Some people, particularly older people, feel that these tools aren't for them.

They are too new-fangled. This is a really limiting mindset. It's not true: these tools are liberating. 'It's never too late to learn' is an alternative and powerful mindset to adopt.

THE VCR SYNDROME

This syndrome refers to the fact that in many families the parents can't program the video and leave it to their children to do. The more comfortable the children become with it, the more the parents leave it to them so they never learn how to do it.

One problem with videos is that some are unsuitable for children. A V-chip – violence chip – has been developed that can be put on the machine to censor out films unsuitable for children.

But the V-chip will not work in practice because children are more adept at finding a way round it than parents are at installing it. Parents have surrendered control to their children because they haven't kept up with the times.

Don't reject new tools: get on top of them. They are easy. Some of them are being taught to eight-year-old children. It's never too late to learn.

Six-hat thinking

Redefine some of your current group sessions, called meetings, as joint thinking sessions. Then adopt a tool called six-hat thinking, originated by Edward de Bono.

Six-hat thinking is so easy to do – yet so effective – that it can be explained in just a few words. The purpose is to get everyone thinking on the same wavelength at the same time, then to switch to another wavelength in an organized way. The technique cures most meeting diseases at a stroke.

This is the opposite of what probably happens in your meetings currently. One person probably makes a suggestion based on facts. Another may use an anecdote from their previous experience to suggest something else. Another gives the arguments against. Someone comes in with facts in support. Someone else comes in with a comment based on gut feel. Someone else asks for order in the process.

And then there are the habitual practices. Person A always sticks to the facts. Person B feels that Person A is too theoretical so always counters their facts with a comment based on their own judgement or experience. Person C always finds fault with what Person D says. Person E always supports Person C and so on and so on.

Six-hat thinking cuts through this mayhem.

In this technique you put on a different thinking hat to do each of six different types of thinking. You declare that you are putting on a particular hat; you may be asked to put on a particular hat for a short time; you can get the whole group to wear one hat for a time then switch together to another. The six hats are:

White: Seek facts, figures, information

Red: Give comments from emotions, feelings, hunches, intuition

Black: Comment about caution, judgement, why it will not work, dangers to watch out for, negatives

Yellow: Identify advantages, benefits, why it is good to do

Green: Suggest alternatives, different ideas, exploration, new ideas, points of interest that form half-ideas, new leads

Blue: Control the process, the purpose, deciding who puts on which hat and when

---

Maybe you think that it looks too simple? That's just a limiting mindset. Instead, adopt the mindset that this is powerful new technology for your cranial computer. Presumably you think nothing of using a mobile phone, nothing of using a satellite dish, nothing of using e-mail, nothing of surfing the Internet.

Organizations using six-hat thinking can dramatically shorten meeting time, because waste is eliminated, and achieve substantially better results at the same time. Where before the habit was to book meetings for one hour, or two hours for a significant meeting, now they find they need to schedule only 20 or 30 minutes for meetings that are dramatically more effective.

Mindmapping

EXERCISE 1

Could you name 50 birds in three minutes?

EXERCISE 2

You are running a conference for 1000 people. Your guest speaker is late, very late. Five minutes before the appointed time for his speech he isn't there. You are suddenly told there is no alternative, you will have to speak to those 1000 people in five minutes' time, for 30 minutes on a subject of your choice.

Choose a subject and decide what you will say. You have only five minutes to plan the speech.

A SOLUTION TO EXERCISE 1

Many people freeze at this exercise. For many, it seems impossible to get anywhere near naming 50 birds in three minutes. Some people don't even try when faced with a discontinuous goal – they give up before they've started. Others start making a list but dry up well before 50.

Here is an alternative approach. Put the problem in a circle in the middle of the page. Then consider for 10–20 seconds the birds that come immediately to mind. Consider what themes or patterns these follow. For example, think about the situations or places in which you encounter birds. As a situation comes to mind, put it on a branch coming from the circle. For example, you might put down garden, house and then remember zoo.

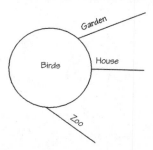

Then consider the birds in each place and write them in as sub-branches. As you think of birds, some will remind you of other situations. When you think of a new theme or situation write in a new branch.

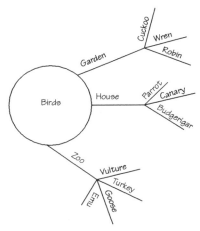

For example, thinking of the zoo brings up vulture and turkey. This in turn triggers a different thought – the theme of birds you eat. Put in a branch. An emu triggers a theme of big birds. Put in a branch. Robin triggers small. Big birds trigger swan, which in turn triggers a theme 'round water'. Put in a branch.

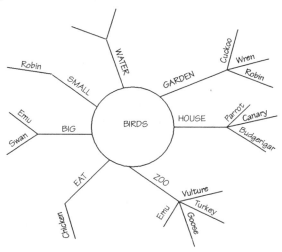

Now tackle each branch and add subbranches as birds come to mind under each theme. Don't worry about duplication, just write. Add more branches as you need to. Even with the branches already identified, you will probably easily get to 50 birds.

A SOLUTION TO EXERCISE 2

Follow a similar process for writing your speech. Put your over-all subject in a circle in the centre.

For example, it may be 'My learnings from living around the world'. You could then have a branch for each place you have lived, with subbranches for topics as they come to mind.

Moreover, as you generate the topics for each place, certain themes will come to mind – such as education and lifestyle – that provide interest through viewing these themes across all the locations. For each such theme, draw another branch and build up that theme as you go.

Assume now that you have the time to go to your photo album and take out a photo of each place you have lived. The photo would bring back a flood of memories that would trigger things in your mind about your experience that you would otherwise not have remembered. Similarly, things happen when you draw a small picture in addition to a word. As we have said before, a picture really does equal a thousand words.

We can learn several things from these exercises:

➤ When you start to think, your mind goes off at tangents. A linear approach to thinking views tangents as distracting. A map approach allows you to capture them and return to the main theme.

➤ When you start to think, one idea triggers another. The linear approach of memo writing can't handle this well because it is simultaneously concerned with how to organize and structure the thoughts in the memo presentation.

➤ When you think your mind spots themes between concrete events as well as learnings and linkages. A linear approach can't handle these easily. A map approach can.

➤ Pictures are powerful triggers for your mind. A traditional approach eliminates pictures. A map approach encourages them.

➤ Color is also a wonderful trigger. A black and white, linear memo approach precludes this. A colored map approach encourages it.

How to mindmap

Mindmapping was invented and developed by Tony Buzan. It is best approached in the following way:

➤ Turn the page sideways.
➤ Put a picture or symbol in the middle of the page (access to right brain) to represent what you want to think about.
➤ Use several colors (also helps access the right brain).
➤ As your thoughts come, draw a branch out from the centre. Put one word on the branch. Add a picture or visual clue. Use different colors for different branches.
➤ As ideas come, add them as secondary, smaller branches on the main branches, like a tree.
➤ Link ideas and thoughts between branches using connecting arrows, asterisks, symbols, numbers, colors, underlining or whatever.
➤ As you do a mindmap different linkages will occur to you, different themes, different ways to approach the subject. You can always do another mindmap using these new branches or linkages if it helps you sort things out in your mind.

The advantages of this method of working compared to the linear, list, preparing-a-memo method are clear:

➤ your whole brain is engaged
➤ you can note things in the right place as they occur to you
➤ one idea triggers another
➤ all sorts of things come into your mind and you can capture them
➤ you can go back, forward and sideways in your thought processes
➤ it's fun and mind opening rather than being a chore.

All this is impossible if you try to write things out in the way you would write a memo. This stops creativity and bogs down the flow of imagination and expression as you are simultaneously planning the outline and considering grammar and structure.

Mindmapping is hugely powerful technology for your cranial computer. It can bring breakthrough effectiveness in thinking about the problem, in summarizing your thoughts or knowledge, as an *aide mémoire* for a presentation instead of notes or a written script. It is already widely used by students as a way of note taking and for revision.

It can be used on your own or in meetings. In meetings, it allows for a period of individual thinking. It then allows a constructive way of sharing that thinking: others need to seek first to understand your mindmap and to have theirs understood. It's terrific technology for building ideas, for getting the very best out of individual minds and then out of those minds working together.

Mindsoftware think pads

A mindmap is a piece of mental software. There are other pieces of Mindsoftware which will help generate step-change performance.

The origins of Mindsoftware can be traced to a similar period as the start of software for the personal computer. PCs started to become popular in the early 1980s and have since been hugely commercialized, as has their software. In the early 1980s, as we saw in Chapter 7, Sperry and Ormstein received a Nobel prize for their work on the brain – the cranial computer. Mindsoftware is software to get the most out of that computer.

Parchment and quill pen software

What is the current status of the cranial software available to you? When they want to do some thinking, most people pick up a pen and a blank, lined, single-color writing pad. What we write on has hardly changed since the days of parchment and the quill pen. We need to make it obsolete because it suffers from two problems: it's boring and it's blank.

It's boring

The parchment and quill pen system is single color, which is single tone, which is monotone, which is monotonous, boring your brains out. Everything else has gone from black and white to colorful in a way that excites the whole brain: from television, video cameras, video games, computer screens, computer software, photographs, and business presentations to photocopies.

It's blank

When we sit at our personal computers to do a task, we expect to be able to get immediate access to a program to help us with that task. We would object to being faced with a blank screen. Moreover, we expect the computer to show us a menu of the software available and lead us through the programs. Yet, out of habit, we accept blank pads to write on.

Mindsoftware

In contrast, Mindsoftware think pads will give you a piece of thinking software to work at on every page, each tied in with tri△ngular thinking strategies. And they will trigger your whole brain through visuals and color.

These are not 'slogan' pads: they are active tools. These are not screen-savers: they are interactive software for the cranial computer.

Mindsoftware pads will not just achieve individual breakthrough results, they can also help spread good habits throughout the organization. Consider what would happen if you changed all your writing pads to Mindsoftware think pads. At a stroke, you would influence the thinking strategies of every person, every meeting, every review, every presentation, every desk, every office.

Moreover, they make it legitimate for each and every individual to refer to them, at any stage, and say: 'Let's apply this strategy'.

Examples of Mindsoftware think pads are given at the end of this book, although unfortunately not in the colors they are normally available.

After one month spent writing on these pads, you'll have transformed your results. You will never want to return to quill pen and blank parchment. They are a breakthrough way to help achieve breakthrough results, relatively easily.

Over 30 replacements for traditional meetings and memos

As we have seen, continuing with your traditional habits and practices for meetings and memos will at best achieve incremental improvements. Most of them are a waste of your talent and time.

Here are over 30 things you could more usefully do.

In groups

➤ Halve your meeting waste immediately:
  - Don't go
  - Reduce frequency
  - Reduce attendance
  - Reduce duration
  - Stop regular meetings
  - Start/finish at odd times (10.17 to 10.52)
  - Only meet because of an agenda rather than having an agenda because you meet
  - Use a telephone conference instead
  - Combine two meetings in one
  - Schedule an unchangeable stop time – lunch
  - Have a no-seat meeting.

These are very easy. Perhaps each on their own is incremental. But there's absolutely no reason you can't be doing all 'easy 11' actively and energetically, now. And that would cut by 50 percent the time and talent you're absorbing in traditional meetings. Do them from tomorrow.

➤ Redefine meetings as joint thinking sessions.

➤ More 'arrow of breakthrough' time in meetings, less 'box of incrementalism'.

➤ Use six-hat thinking for joint thinking sessions.

➤ Use six-hat thinking individually.

➤ Use the 'act in the action zone' model to check whether you are in the action zone or in areas of trouble; and whether you're working on the biggest scope of the problem.

➤ Each person mindmaps their own ideas individually to start with then shares them round the group. This forces questions from other people before they can fully understand your meaning. It promotes building on half-ideas.

➤ Do a 'plus/minus interesting' mindmap on your own. Identify all the positives, all the negatives and all the other interesting points that may be relevant. Then collate your results with others'.

➤ Get an on-site 'off-site room'. Call it a 'joint thinking room' rather than a meeting room.

On your own

➤ Halve your memo waste immediately:
  - Don't write, talk
  - Don't write, call
  - Wait and see
  - Copy few people, if any
  - Shorten memos to reduce points of possible contention
  - Skim, don't study
  - Throw out, don't copy on or file
  - Handwrite the answer on the original
  - Don't respond
  - Don't send on, put in the wastepaper bin
  - Return with comment: 'Not needed'.

➤ Work through the arrow of breakthrough.

➤ Think on your own out of the box.

➤ Do a six-hat mindmap. Map out all the points that come to mind under each of De Bono's six thinking hats.

➤ Do a 'to-do' map.

➤ Do a plus/minus interesting mindmap.

➤ Identify the boundaries, then play with them.

➤ Work out how to make your tacit knowledge explicit to others in order to build knowhow.

➤ Seek out explicit knowledge on your issue to build knowhow.

➤ Engage with another tacit knowledge holder on the issue to build knowhow.

As you can see, there are many, many better things to do than continuing with your current habits and practices.

Last, but not least, take time to 'get on fire' to help charge yourself up so you will be able to break out of the box of incrementalism and aim for step-change goals.

Getting on fire is the last thinking strategy.

The Eighth
Thinking Strategy

Recharge yourself, get on fire

versus

Ever harder, longer

10 *Getting on Fire*

The mind is not a vessel to be filled, but a fire to be ignited.

Plutarch

Get on fire and help others around you to get on fire! This is the sort of attitude and environment that will help you bring all the other strategies into vibrant life towards step-change results.

Don't stay happily in the rut of the status quo, stuck in the box of incrementalism. Think big instead. Go for step-change results.

The problem that most individuals and organizations face is that they can only keep up this sort of attitude for a short time. They get fired up, possibly following a seminar, a presentation or a course. But after a short time people are sucked back into the box of routine, back into the habits of a lifetime, back into boring normality.

Despite your best intentions, there seem to be too many day-to-day issues, problems and concerns to bring you down. All too soon you are back to routine days, routine habits and practices; having a few good days but also lots of bad days; trapped by worries and concerns.

How do you and the organization break out of this?

Attitude, energy and sparkle

Getting on fire, and keeping on fire, means achieving and maintaining both a positive attitude and terrific energy, with a wonderfully fresh sparkle. These are difficult to sustain when faced with everyday realities. People and events push you off course, dampen enthusiasm and trigger negative attitudes – and long hours and work overload dampen your sparkle.

Consider the following grid of low to high on attitude and energy:

➤ Those with low energy and poor attitude can be typified as 'deadbeats'.
➤ Those with high energy but poor attitude can be called 'cynics'.
➤ Those with good attitude but low energy can be described as 'politicians'.
➤ Those with a great attitude combined with high energy are 'winners'.

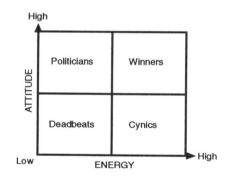

Many people reading this book may feel that they can rightly position themselves in the winners' quadrant. But is it really a step-change, breakthrough objective to aim at being in the winners' quadrant – or even to have your whole organization in the winners' quadrant? That's a fairly incremental goal.

The breakthrough goal is to get in the very best, top 1 percent area of the winners' quadrant; and to get your whole organization there – with a sparkle!

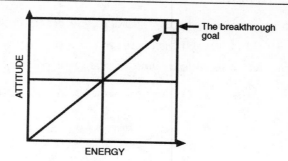

What are the tools and techniques to get into and stay in the best 1 percent area? How can you get and stay on fire?

And what are the tools and techniques to do this in the face of what appear to be ever-increasing hurdles? The hurdle of downsizing has often led to overload, to longer and longer hours on treadmill activities. The hurdle of the pressures of modern life — with an ever-increasing need for family time outside work — conflicts with the growing encroachment of the job into all hours through modern communications and their accessibility at home.

It is difficult to get and stay in the very top 1 percent area of ceaseless energy and great attitude, with a sustained wonderful sparkle. You need to take action to move yourself higher and higher up the attitude and energy axes all the way to the top right-hand corner.

There now follows a smorgasbord of tips, tools and techniques to achieve this and help others do the same. Choose the ones that are right for you. Aim for 1 percent improvement a day. You'll have doubled your effectiveness in a couple of months. Make these techniques second nature — like riding a bike, playing the piano or driving a car.

The perpetual circle of energy, attitude and sparkle

These are four key quadrants of your day in which to take action. Together they form a 24-hour circle of energy, attitude and sparkle.

Each reinforces the other, and keeps you going. Taking action in any one area will step-change your and the organization's effectiveness. Taking action in all four will supercharge it.

THE PERPETUAL CIRCLE OF ENERGY, ATTITUDE AND SPARKLE

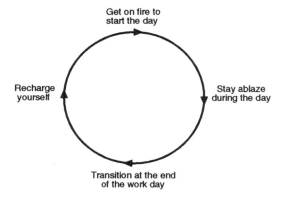

Recharge yourself

You can recharge yourself by taking a break. So holidays are good, as are long weekends. If you're not already doing it, do something each evening to help you relax.

Resting periodically from what you do will help, but it won't get you up to that top-class 1 percent on attitude and energy. It may rest and refresh you somewhat, but it won't go all the way to recharging you and getting you on fire.

You generally get on fire by gaining fulfillment outside work, rather than using time outside work to get a rest or relief from work. There is a huge difference between these two approaches.

And you can only get terrific fulfillment if you know the balance of goals you want to achieve across all areas of your life and are taking action to achieve them. Then you'll be satisfied with your whole life, gaining energy from each part of it to put towards the next part.

If your work is your whole life, it can be shown in a box like the one opposite.

MY WHOLE LIFE

```
┌─────────────┐
│             │
│             │
│    WORK     │
│             │
│             │
└─────────────┘
```

Imagine that your work is taken away from you, perhaps by redundancy or retirement. Or that your satisfaction from work is taken away because you feel unappreciated or are passed over for promotion. What does your whole life look and feel like now?

MY WHOLE LIFE

```
┌─────────┐
│         │
│         │
│         │
└─────────┘
```

The answer is empty. You become empty, depressed, energyless.

By contrast, think about your life as a grid. For each area on the grid, have your mind think about one area separately and single-mindedly, with 100 percent energy and commitment, then switch it to another area.

MY WHOLE LIFE

Family	Work	Hobby
Partner	Alone time	Sport
Pleasure	Health	Friends

Doesn't applying your mind in this way make your life fuller and give you more energy?

If your work were to be taken away from you now, what would your life look like?

MY WHOLE LIFE

Family		Hobby
Partner	Alone time	Sport
Pleasure	Health	Friends

The other areas become a source of energy that recharges your batteries and can bring you into work on fire, ready to fix whatever's going wrong in your job.

You'll get maximum energy for your job and your life when you are actively working on achieving a balance of goals across the broad areas of your life – the balance that is particularly right for you.

Outside the work day

What happens outside the work day undoubtedly affects what happens within it. This is an inescapable and, for some, uncomfortable truth.

Think of the many examples of this:

➤ Many people find that physical exercise, jogging or working out in a gym, helps clear the mind.

➤ In many educational systems, all-rounders do well. Moving from one sphere to focus on another helps achievement in both spheres. A change does seem to be as good as a rest.

➤ Successful people seem to have more energy for more and more things: 'if you want something done, ask a busy person'. Doing things outside of work, far from draining them, seems to give them extra energy.

WHEN DO YOU GET YOUR BEST IDEAS?

Get together in a group. Ask people to call out what they tend to be doing when they get their best ideas. Write down or map out the answers you get.

Typical answers will be: when walking the dog; in the shower or bath; gardening; shaving; driving the car; jogging; listening to music; in the middle of the night.

What do they all have in common? None of them is at work. Ideas on work often come outside work.

There are technical reasons for this to do with the brain wave-band that our minds are in on different occasions during the day. We tend to use lower-frequency, creative brainwaves outside work and our mind works subconsciously on the problems or opportunities we face at work. In the normal, hectic patterns of work, we are driven into higher-frequency waves that make creativity more difficult.

There is an inextricable link between life in work and life outside work. What you do at work will affect your life outside; what you do outside will affect your life at work.

What you do outside can not only bring satisfaction in itself, it can bring you into work on fire. And staying on fire at work can allow you to do things outside work with a completely different zest and attitude.

Success as an energy source

What is success? Success is choosing the balance of what you want, then taking action to achieve it. It is as much to do with choosing to avoid being a complete failure in one aspect of your life that is important to you — perhaps family, children, a relationship, health, personal fulfillment — as it is with getting to the top in another area of your life.

The balance you need will differ from person to person. And, moreover, what any one person wants at 20 is not the same as the balance you want at 30 or at 40.

It's fine to be exclusively single-minded in your choice of balance — as long as you make a choice. Don't continue with an unsatisfactory, energyless balance just because it's your habit. Reinvent your choice. Don't continue because you're simply doing what you think is expected of you or what you've always done, without enough questioning.

Don't spend your life climbing a ladder only to find it's resting on the wrong wall.

Don't get on the bus of your life each day. Be the driver of the bus.

Most people spend longer planning their annual holiday than they do planning their life. Make sure that you plan yours.

Consider the following exercises to identify the goals and action you want.

MINDMAP A WISH, WANT AND DREAM LIST

Put on each main branch of the map the areas of most interest and concern to you: work, your partner, each family member, leisure, friends, health, self-development, learning, sport etc. Branch out into things you'd like to achieve in each area. Then branch out to action you can take – today.

LIGHTNING WILL STRIKE

Assume that you know lightning is going to strike you dead in six months' time. Mindmap what you would do in those six months.

FUNERAL ORATION

Imagine a 30-minute oration at your funeral. Mindmap what you'd like to be said about you at the end of your life. Then mindmap ways to achieve it.

Taking action in these areas will help you recharge yourself and get on fire.

Get on fire to start the day

Most people start the day in neutral. Whether it turns out to be a good day or a bad day depends on what happens to them. If things get off to a poor start, they can quickly go from bad to worse.

Sometimes it can be things as trivial as a misunderstanding at breakfast, a poor journey into work, some rudeness on the part of others or some minor disappointment in the early mail.

What a ridiculous approach! To get breakthrough results, you need to take positive action to make the day a great day. Many people wish each other 'Good morning'. Others tell people 'Have a nice day'. But few take action at the start of the day to make it a great day.

Decide and plan how to make your day wonderful. Consider all the actions you can take, across the broad area of the goals you're working on, to move things ahead in the directions you want.

And don't do this in a half-brained, logical way. Use a whole-brained approach. Generate some power and passion for the day. Get excited about the carrot of what you can achieve. And get dissatisfied through the crippling stick of today being a boring, routine repetition of hundreds of days before that you've lived through rather than lived – one more checked off on the way to death.

Overleaf is some whole-brained stimulation to start you off. Then create your own.

Staying ablaze during the work day

Any fire will die if it doesn't get a steady replenishment of fuel. And every fire needs to avoid having too much cold water thrown on it.

So it is with your fire of brilliant energy and attitude. It requires attention to stay ablaze. More fuel is needed during the work day. And you know in advance that organizational life is such that there will be lots of cold water around to stop you staying ablaze.

GET IN A GOOD SPIRIT FOR THE DAY

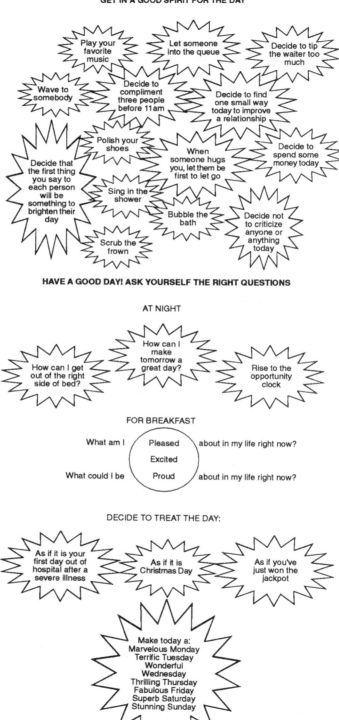

Play your favorite music

Let someone into the queue

Decide to tip the waiter too much

Wave to somebody

Decide to compliment three people before 11am

Decide to find one small way today to improve a relationship

Polish your shoes

When someone hugs you, let them be first to let go

Decide to spend some money today

Decide that the first thing you say to each person will be something to brighten their day

Sing in the shower

Bubble the bath

Decide not to criticize anyone or anything today

Scrub the frown

HAVE A GOOD DAY! ASK YOURSELF THE RIGHT QUESTIONS

AT NIGHT

How can I get out of the right side of bed?

How can I make tomorrow a great day?

Rise to the opportunity clock

FOR BREAKFAST

What am I   Pleased   about in my life right now?

Excited

What could I be   Proud   about in my life right now?

DECIDE TO TREAT THE DAY:

As if it is your first day out of hospital after a severe illness

As if it is Christmas Day

As if you've just won the jackpot

Make today a:
Marvelous Monday
Terrific Tuesday
Wonderful Wednesday
Thrilling Thursday
Fabulous Friday
Superb Saturday
Stunning Sunday

There are four key areas to focus on to keep ablaze during the work day:

➤ Insist on doing only the most important things.
➤ Celebrate not doing other things.
➤ Focus on the three levels of satisfaction: the achievement, the learning and the experience.
➤ Manage your moods.

Insist on doing only the most important things

This is the single most important way to stay ablaze and get step-change results. If there was one thing to do, and only one thing, this would be it.

Mindmap the most important things for you to do to achieve your goals. Then focus on these relentlessly. That's all.

MIND-OPENING PRACTICE: ROCKS IN A BARREL

Consider the following exercise, first developed by Stephen Covey.

An empty barrel is put on a table. Four big rocks are put into it.

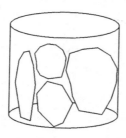

Sand is poured in between the rocks. The barrel is shaken and more sand is poured in. It is shaken again and more sand can be fitted in.

Now some very, very fine sand is added. Some can get in, fitting in the little gaps between the coarser sand particles.

The barrel is shaken. More goes in.

Finally, water is poured in, allowed to soak down and more is poured in. The barrel is now absolutely full.

What can we learn from this mind-opener? Many people say that it shows how much can be fitted in if you really try.

But that's not the main lesson. The main lesson is: if you don't put the four rocks in at the beginning, how will you ever get them in?

Celebrate not doing other things

The issue for most people and organizations is often not identifying the most important things: it is finding a way to focus on them without getting caught up in other things.

Step-change results will come from focus on only the most important things. Incrementalism will be the result if you give time and focus to the other things.

10 thoughts about not doing other things

1   The enemy of success is the worthwhile
2   The only person who got everything done by Friday was Robinson Crusoe

3 Perfectionism is not a virtue, it's a disease
4 It needs doing – but by others
5 Focus on being effective rather than efficient
6 Junk junk
7 Use the LBW drawer
8 Dance to your own tune
9 Celebrate five no-nos or five ways to say no
10 Decide to finish for the day and celebrate it

The enemy of success is the worthwhile

Don't continually spend your time enthusiastically doing things that will help. Or doing things that seem worthwhile, but overlooking the fact that they are clogging up your life and stopping you having time for the things that are really most important.

The only person who got everything done by Friday was Robinson Crusoe

You can't do everything, but you can do the most important things.

Perfectionism is not a virtue, it's a disease

Are you a perfectionst? Do you want to change this typo? Don't spend 50 percent of your time on a project trying to get the last 10 percent of value.

It needs doing – but by others

➤ Decide what others can do for you and set them on to it.
➤ Delegate and operate to the motto: 'I only do what only I can do.'
➤ Delegate. Remember that your pupil can't fly solo if you want to stay in the plane.
➤ What's the best use of my time, right now? Ask and ask again.

Focus on being effective rather than efficient

Efficiency is doing things right. Effectiveness is doing the right things. Do the right things right and leave the rest.

Junk junk

Don't generate junk:

➤ Use the WPB: wastepaper basket.
➤ 95 percent of what gets filed never gets looked at again.
➤ Do the junk mail test.

Use the LBW drawer

Fill the 'let the bumph wait' drawer. Fill it up and celebrate it being full rather than worrying about it. When it's full, pass it to the WPB (wastepaper basket) and fill it up again.

Dance to your own tune

Don't dance to the tune of the telephone ringing, the e-mail message, the voicemail, the interrupting colleague. The average person gets interrupted seven times an hour, once every eight minutes. Don't be average.

Celebrate five no-nos or five ways to say 'no'

➤ Refuse early, before people build an expectation that you may agree.
➤ Be polite and pleasant.
➤ Give reasons why not.
➤ Indicate that you are choosing to do other things instead.
➤ Offer an alternative suggestion on how the person might get help.

Decide to finish for the day and celebrate it

➤ Stop for the day after you've done the most important things. Don't go on with busy, busy work, just to feel you're filling in a certain number of long hours at your job. Instead, go and recharge your batteries and come into work again on fire.

➤ Try a 5 o'clock finish to the day, if you normally work until 6 or 7 or even 8. Announce very early that you're going to leave at 5 and broadcast it widely. One 5 o'clock day is worth it even if for the rest of the week you have to work to 9 o'clock to make up.

➤ On the other hand, don't feel pressured to do differently if longer, harder switches you on. Or switches you on for a period in your life when you want to immerse yourself in work. Every organization needs its fair share of people who want to go harder, longer, to stay competitive. They bring different things to the party.

Staying ablaze

Whatever activity you are engaged in, there are three levels of satisfaction that together produce further energy and fire:

➤ The level of achievement – succeeding in the task.
➤ The level of experience – smelling the roses you find as you go about the task.
➤ The level of learning – learning while you go about the task.

Too many people focus on just one level – more often than not on achievement. But this misses out on the huge value of taking action simultaneously in the other two levels: of enjoying the experience as you go through it; of learning what you can from the activity as you go through it.

Taking action equally at all three levels not only provides ceaseless energy but also gives you your best chance of achievement. The three levels form a broad triangle.

Focusing on achievement alone forms a narrow, brittle triangle. It's single-minded but brittle and prone to crack under pressure – because there's no learning to get it back on track, no love of the experience to give it a broad base of perspective. And a focus on either of the other two levels in isolation is equally fragile. Do all three and you'll find greater energy and fire to help achieve step-change results.

Manage your mood

Your best intentions at staying ablaze can be offset in an instant by cold water being thrown on the fire. You need tips and techniques to manage your mood so you can stop becoming down for too long when something negative happens. Don't just do it logically, do it in a whole-brained way. Here are some suggestions.

15 ways to manage your mood

Unjust remark

When an unjust remark is made, imagine that the person making it is drunk – the remark is slurred, stooopid, ridiculous – and smile.

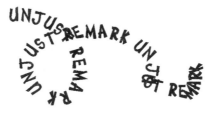

Unfair comment

When something unfair is written, imagine how small it really is. Imagine it on a piece of paper in front of you. Rise above it from your seat, all the way to the ceiling. Can you even see it from there?

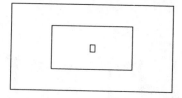

Look how small and insignificant it truly is.

Troubles

When you have troubles, imagine sitting down in an armchair and writing each on a separate piece of paper. Then see yourself piling the papers on the floor and setting light to them. Doesn't that feel better?

Bad feelings

Everyone on the planet has bad feelings. They are not unique, not your own personal tragedy. So when you get one, just tick the box like you would a questionnaire. I've got:

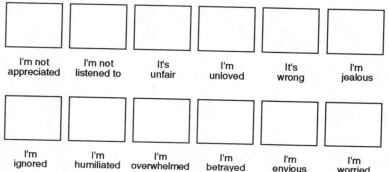

Tick the box, recognize the feeling and move on to dealing with it and replacing it with a better feeling.

Soap opera

Your life's a soap opera and not even as good as the ones on television. When you get bad feelings, just think of the theme to a soap opera – *Neighbours*, *The Archers*, *EastEnders*, *Coronation Street*, *Dynasty* or *Melrose Place*. Play the tune in your mind and smile.

Unreal

We often interpret an event, a glance or a remark in a way that was never intended to give us that feeling. We see slights, innuendos and messages that are not intended and get unduly upset by them.

Are there any triangles here?

When you perceive slights, most often you are seeing something that isn't really there and wasn't intended.

Sing the blues

Make your own list of songs which describe your blues. Sing them to yourself and smile.

I heard it through the grapevine
Breaking up is hard to do
Baby please don't let me be misunderstood
I shall be released
You're so good, you're so good, baby,
      you're so good

A different way to look at it

Always find a different, better way to look at things. Which of these lines are parallel?

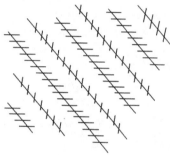

You will probably conclude that alternative lines are parallel. Now turn the book sideways, put your nose down on the paper and look along the lines. They are all parallel. Always choose a different, better way to look at it.

Top 10 feelings

Get yourself one of the top ten feelings in the world! My suggestions are overleaf.

Write down all the things you can think of that would justify having one of these feelings. And then have that feeling.

TOP 10 FEELINGS

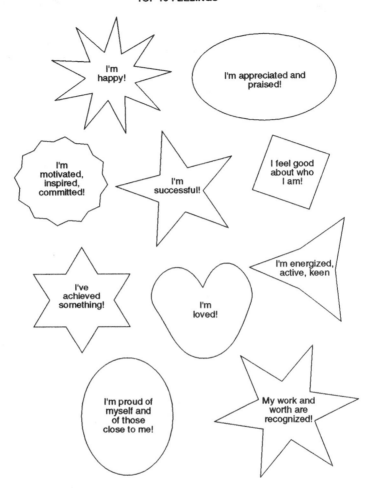

Choose a fame frame

Feel good about yourself. Imagine yourself being adored and adulated.

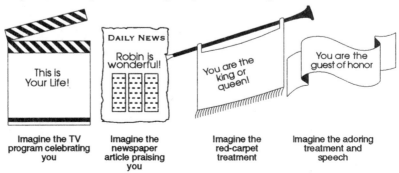

Laugh about it in the future – now

We'll look back and laugh at this:

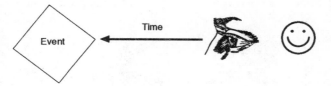

So do it now.

Focus on afterwards

When faced with an unpleasant task or difficulty, focus on how great you'll feel afterwards:

Recognize a 'splatt!'

Call it out for what it is. That's a John-splatt! That's a wife-splatt! That's a boss-splatt! That's a person-splatt! We all do splatts. We don't really mean them harmfully. When they happen, break the ice by calling them out and laughing at them.

Buy a gift in your mind

Choose a gift for a particular person, now, in your mind. What would you give, where could you get it? What would bring a smile to their face?

Smile more

Transition at the end of the work day

It would be stupid to do all this during the work day and then come home and have a bummer of an evening. Yet we often end up having bad evenings. Why?

The transition time between work and non-work is vitally important to maintaining energy, attitude and sparkle. We do this reentry about 240 times a year. But we rarely sit back to work out how to do it brilliantly. Instead, the mood can be decided by happenstance, by the first few things said or unsaid, the first piece of body language correctly or incorrectly interpreted, the first things done or not done, the first look on your face, intended or unintended, the first mood-suggesting action or omission.

The transition at the end of the day is far more important than the transition at the beginning of the day, from sleep to work. At the beginning of the day you are rested and you are entering a part of the day that has action and busyness as a routine.

The opposite is true at the end of the work day. You are tired and are entering a period where there is not necessarily a routine of action and busyness. How your transition goes will dictate how much energy-giving activity you'll engage in that evening.

So work out your best transition tools when asked 'How was your day?' Be ready to give a short summary of your stories; avoid the need for mind-reading; be balanced in what you say; set it up to talk about later; respond with empathy rather than logic.

This is the final part of the 'perpetual circle'. Get discontinuously great at it. Here are some whole-brained tips.

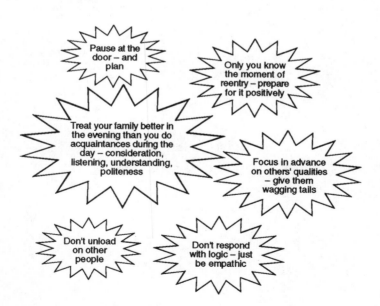

Pause at the door – and plan

Only you know the moment of reentry – prepare for it positively

Treat your family better in the evening than you do acquaintances during the day – consideration, listening, understanding, politeness

Focus in advance on others' qualities – give them wagging tails

Don't unload on other people

Don't respond with logic – just be empathic

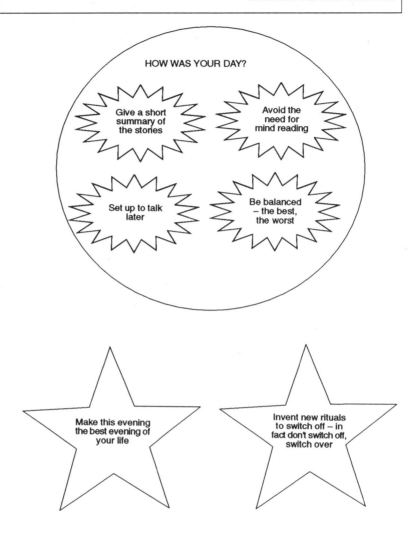

Follow the techniques outlined in this chapter and you will be on your way to recharging yourself and getting on fire.

11 *Breakthrough Results, Relatively Easily*

Now you've read the book, what do you do? How do you put tri△ngular thinking into practice and go beyond the box?

The answer is simple – start to change your thinking habits as you work and get others around you to do the same. That's the way to get breakthrough results, relatively easily.

Your current habits will keep you in the box of incrementalism. If you want to keep on getting what you've always got, then keep on doing what you've always done. Except this won't even get you incremental improvement in the future, because of the rate of change.

Don't aim to change the culture, just aim to change the habits. Start tomorrow doing things differently, doing different things, a little at a time. It's easy because you don't have to change everything at once. Just use 10 percent of these ideas to start with, on 10 percent of your issues, and you'll be amazed at the difference. Start breaking out of the box.

Any strategy is a choice and it's the same with thinking strategies. Most people forget that they actually have a choice of how to think and continue with their current ways out of force of habit. The only habit to develop is the habit of choice.

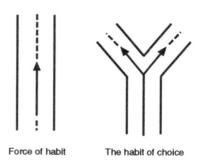

Force of habit   The habit of choice

Many people have a habit of choice on very minor, incremental things. They fail to consider the habit of choice on life-defining things like their thinking strategies.

Thus people are concerned about what clothes to choose for work. At coffee break, they choose their type of coffee, even type of milk to be added and type of sweetener. At lunch break, people consider in some detail which of four or five salad dressings to choose and which sort of bread to choose for the sandwich.

But back at the workplace too many people slip into weak thinking strategies out of force of habit, hardly realizing that there is a choice.

Each of the eight thinking strategies in this book is designed to force a choice between adopting one thinking method and avoiding another.

The best way to change your habits is to use the two operating principles outlined at the beginning of this book.

Use push and pull

Don't just decide what you want to move towards. Decide also that you want to move away from the alternative. Doing both gives you the power to change the habit. Focus on forcing a choice.

Develop both an attraction to what you want to move towards and dissatisfaction with what you want to avoid.

Consider a woman with the objective of running 100 meters very fast. She is motivated by a specific goal, winning a certain race or achieving a specific time. This is pull.

There may be a man who will also run very fast – because he is being chased by a man-killing dog. He may well run a personal best. This is push.

The secret of habit change is to combine the power of these two systems – to use push and pull. Aim to run fast and put a man-killing dog behind you to help.

Use heart and head

You won't change a habit merely through intellectual agreement that it needs doing. You need to generate some passion, some emotion, some commitment. You need to put your heart into it, get yourself on fire.

Use push and pull, heart and head, as you go about changing your thinking habits along the lines of the strategic choices outlined in this book.

Think about choosing to fire the arrow of breakthrough instead of sitting in the box of incrementalism. Think about using tri△ngular thinking instead of vertical or lateral thinking. Think about using pole-vault breakthrough instead of high-jump incrementalism.

Systematically, every day, use more and more of the eight thinking strategies outlined in this book that form the arrow of breakthrough:

Picture a step-change	vs	Happy doing a bit better
Build knowhow	vs	Drown in information
Use creative thinking	vs	Logic alone
Act in the action zone	vs	Act without thinking
Become a whole-brained	vs	Half-brained organization
Choose powerful	vs	Limiting mindsets
Hats, maps and thinking pads	vs	Meetings and memos
Recharge yourself, get on fire	vs	Ever harder, longer

You can start to make these choices from Monday morning – and this will start to transform your results.

You can help your organization transform itself by encouraging each member to read this book and put its ideas into practice.

But if you could change one habit, and one only, what would it be? What could make the biggest difference? What could be the equivalent of the flapping of the butterfly's wing in South America that causes a hurricane in the Atlantic?

In my experience, it would be to give up writing on blank writing pads and move to use Mindsoftware think pads. At a stroke, this would activate each and every one of the above thinking strategies, by providing software for the best computer in the world – your own personal cranial computer.

Examples of Mindsoftware think pads are given in the next few pages. Further information can be obtained from:

Business Beyond the Box
PO Box 85
Beverley
HU17 0YE
UK

Freephone: 0800 4588540

Website: http://www.karoo.net/storm/okeeffe
E-mail: okeeffe@storm.karoo.co.uk

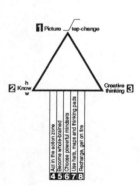

USE TRIANGULAR THINKING

Applying
your
mind
for
THR**R**OUGH
Results

USE TRIANGULAR THINKING

HEART AND HEAD

HEART AND HEAD

♥ & WHAT'S THE LOGIC?   WHERE'S THE PASSION?

1 PICTURE A STEPCHANGE

PICTURE A STEPCHANGE ?

STEP-CHANGE
KNOW-HOW
CREATIVE THINKING

**WHAT'S THE WORD PICTURE
YOU ENVISAGE?**

_____
_____
_____
_____
_____

2
BUILD KNOW-HOW vs DROWN IN INFORMATION

Applying your mind for THR▮OUGH Results

STOP INFORMATION POLLUTION

BUILD KNOW-HOW

Tricks of the trade
Knowhow
Go to the horse's mouth
Inside knowledge
Local knowledge
Know what you are doing
Know your way round
Know the right person

TACIT TO TACIT
_____
_____

TACIT TO EXPLICIT
_____
_____

EXPLICIT TO TACIT
_____
_____

EXPLICIT TO EXPLICIT
_____
_____

3 vs LOGIC ALONE

PLAY WITH BOUNDARIES

vs

PLAY WITHIN THE BOUNDARIES

WHAT BOUNDARIES
ARE WE ACCEPTING?

_____
_____
_____
_____

4 ACT IN THE ACTION ZONE
vs ACT WITHOUT THINKING

Applying your mind for THR**R**OUGH Results

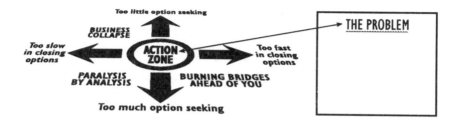

5 BECOME WHOLE-BRAINED
vs HALF-BRAINED

Applying
your
mind
for
THR**R**OUGH
Results

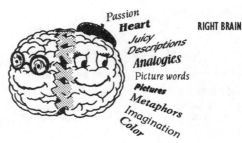

LEFT BRAIN Logic · **RIGHT BRAIN**

Logic
Lists
Numbers
Analysis
Linear
Head
Logic
Lists
Numbers
Analysis
Linear
Head

Passion
Heart
Juicy
Descriptions
Analogies
Picture words
Pictures
Metaphors
Imagination
Color

1234567890

6 CHOOSE POWERFUL MINDSETS
OVER LIMITING MINDSETS

Applying your mind for THR☐OUGH Results

YOU CAN CHOOSE YOUR MINDSET

Many hands make light work	Too many cooks spoil the broth
Better be safe than sorry	Nothing ventured nothing gained
You can only climb a mountain step by step	You can't cross a chasm in two jumps
Can't teach an old dog new tricks	It's never too late to learn

WHAT MINDSETS ARE WE ADOPTING ON THIS ISSUE?

_____

_____

_____

_____